FINDING
THE
MAGIC
IN
MIDDLE
SCHOOL

FINDING THE MAGIC IN MIDDLE SCHOOL

Tapping Into the Power and Potential
of the Middle School Years

CHRIS BALME

zerocirclepress

PACIFICA, CALIFORNIA

Published by Zero Circle Press, Pacifica, California

Cover design by Misa Grannis
Book design by Maureen Forys, Happenstance Type-O-Rama
Cover images inspired by the photography of Mario Alvarez

ISBN: 979-8-9860698-0-7 (paperback)
ISBN: 979-8-9860698-1-4 (ebook)

Names of students portrayed in this book have been changed to protect
their privacy.

This book contains stories and reflections from the author's experience as
co-founder and head of school at Millennium School, a role he held from
2014 to 2020. The author wishes to make clear that this content consists
of his own personal views and that he is no longer formally affiliated with
Millennium School. As Millennium School has continued to evolve, the
views expressed in this book do not necessarily reflect the current methods
or curriculum of Millennium School. Millennium® is a registered trademark
of the Millennium School, which holds all rights in that mark and the other
intellectual property owned by the school. No proceeds from this publication
went to Millennium School. For more information on Millennium School or
its evolving research and methods, see www.millenniumschool.org.

For Stephen Lessard

CONTENTS

INTRODUCTION

"I'll go next," said a quiet voice, and eight sets of jaws dropped to the floor.

I was advising a group of middle school students, a group I'd seen daily since the first day of their sixth-grade year. Now they were older, taller seventh graders, who thought they could predict what each person would say—until now.

One student had remained virtually silent in my advisory for well over a year. Ian had a soft-spoken and kind presence, with large eyes that often seemed to be held wide open. He had a keen sense for the minimum possible statement he could make to shift the attention away from himself and onto the next speaker. For all that we had been getting to know each other, often in profound ways, he remained a mystery.

Until that day. Near the end of our advisory session I had suggested we play a game called Hot Seat, in which students volunteered to receive questions from the rest of the group. It's a way to give their peers permission to ask questions, to reveal their curiosity about each other. And middle schoolers are *very* curious about each other. I knew we had some seasoned Hot Seat players in our group, ready and eager to be asked a personal question.

Then Ian, who had said so little despite a year of invitations, whose responses were normally not only brief but quiet to the point of inaudible, said, "I'll go next," and volunteered to be in the Hot

Seat. With a subtle smile, he turned to the group and showed he was ready for questions. I was so stunned that I stared at him for a second while my mind caught up with reality. I had grown to care deeply about this group, and with those three words, he had made my day. From a quick look around, I could see that his peers were thrilled too.

That day, Ian wanted to be seen by his group. He wanted to relate, to know and be known. There's no more sincere desire at this age, and perhaps at any age. I don't know if he'll remember that day as clearly as I do, but I suspect it marked a turn in his life. After that day he began to open up more to the group, to share what was going on in his life. He was never chatty, but now he was connected.

Middle school often begins with the terrifying realization that you're in a complicated social world, where others watch you closely. This realization can shake you to the core, even lead you to choose silence for a time, as Ian had. But with the right support and safe space, an equally big opportunity emerges: to learn how to be yourself around others. That's what is at stake in these magical years. If we see this potential, we may be able to ask a question that reframes how we think about these curious years of middle school, which so many have learned to dread.

Is middle school the worst time of life—or the worst-understood time?

This book is about the joy, mystery, and potential of this extraordinary time in life, all of which are available when we understand it more deeply. Middle school is about nothing less than discovering who you are, and what you can do, in a social world.

But let's acknowledge the elephant in the room: the words "middle school" inspire dread in most parents, even in the general population. Middle school teachers are used to receiving shocked or pitying looks when they say what they do for work. We associate these years with social drama or even trauma, lost years of academic growth, and prickly tween attitudes.

Some of these fears are well placed. The research shows that all too often, middle school is when academic engagement plunges, conflict at home increases, mental health problems emerge, and bullying, exclusion, and other forms of social harm are inflicted. But this is not how the middle school years have to be. This is just how we've become accustomed to doing them.

The question that motivates this book is: what *could* the middle school years be? If we understood the potential and transformative processes of this phase, what would happen? This is not to say that we can make everything smooth sailing—any time of such rapid personal growth will have awkward and clumsy moments. But middle school does *not* have to be traumatic. And it does *not* have to involve disengaging from school or turning against parents. In fact, this is a time of magic.

This book is an invitation to an adventure in search of that magic. The magic is in the transformation from child to adult, a journey that begins in earnest during middle school. We'll see things through middle school eyes, drawing on neuroscience, psychology, and developmental science. As we see the drives at play and develop more understanding for what it's like to *be* a middle schooler, we'll be able to interpret their behavior more accurately and often more positively. We'll be able to work *with* the developmental drives middle schoolers feel, rather than falling into the trap of fighting their natural motivations.

It's worth noting that the human brain goes through two periods of particularly rapid development in our lifetimes: the first from birth to age five, and the second in early adolescence (roughly the middle school years). There is a wealth of books and other resources to help us navigate the early-childhood years, offering excellent understandings of the development at play. Parents of young children depend on this guidance. For many it would be hard to imagine making it through those years without some knowledge of what's going on developmentally.

But where is the equivalent for early adolescence, that other time of massive change, with all the difficulty and opportunity such change provides? There has been too little written for this age, and perhaps it is not surprising, then, that we often miss the developmental trends in middle school or end up at our wits' end after battling them. This book is an attempt to spare us that grief and to provide the developmental guidance so that we can understand, appreciate, and simply enjoy the experience of raising or teaching middle schoolers.

In addition to developmental knowledge, we adults need one very special ally to help us navigate this terrain: our own adolescent self. They're still in there, after all. We don't evolve by erasing old versions of ourselves. We are more like trees, evolving by adding rings of growth around the core. In this sense, our middle school self is still present, alive and well, and closer to the heart of us than many aspects of our current-day adult self. In case this middle schooler is not often visited, as is the case for many of us who would rather forget the difficulties or confusions of those years, we will need to find them. It will be up to us to bring them out of hiding and consult them for advice, to hire them as a trustworthy advisor for our journey with the students or children in our lives.

Where We're Going

Part 1 of this book is our foundation: the core understanding of adolescent development that informs every choice we make as parents and teachers. With understanding comes greater ability to love. We can avoid taking things personally and can see even adolescents' most aggravating moments as a sincere effort to accomplish their developmental tasks. We'll learn how to align ourselves with these tasks, so that we are helping middle schoolers accomplish their deepest goals rather than battling them.

Here we'll answer questions like:

* *What are the greatest developmental needs of middle schoolers?*

* *Why are some middle schoolers obsessed with friends above all else, while others care most about grades and achievement, and still others seem to believe that grades don't matter much at all?*

* *Should I be worried if my child constantly experiments with their identity?*

* *How and why does the parent–child relationship shift in middle school?*

* *How can I help my middle schooler take on more responsibility and understand the "real world" better?*

In part 2, we'll face an open secret about parenting adolescents: their transformation is an invitation, or sometimes a demand, for us to transform as well. If we want to be of greatest service, we will need to evolve our parenting style, maybe even face some demons from our own adolescent years, and commit to being fellow learners alongside them.

At the heart of many of the techniques and mindsets for parents is the ability to model being an adult who is aware, authentic, and open-minded. You do not need to be superhuman—in fact, that is exactly what is *not* needed. To be yourself, imperfect and always growing, often through difficulty—this is who middle schoolers need to see.

We'll answer questions that many parents hold, such as:

* *What is social-emotional intelligence, and how can I help my child develop in this area?*

* *What are the physical habits or practices that will help my child manage their emotions and focus more in school?*

* *What are the qualities of a great middle school?*

* *How do I handle some of the common challenges of middle school, like requests for phones and access to social media?*

* *Beyond school, which activities are most important for adolescent growth and development?*

In part 3, we'll explore what makes a great middle school. How can we make a place deserving of the humans-in-transformation who walk its halls? We'll consider how to build advisory programs that foster belonging and deep social-emotional learning. We'll reimagine the role of teacher into that of a guide and examine how educators can reach into this role. We'll discover more effective approaches to academics, using projects and real-world problems to make learning engaging and memorable.

For educators, part 3 offers both big and small steps toward these goals. We'll answer questions like:

* *How can I become confident and skilled as an advisory facilitator?*

* *How can I use project-based learning, even within a traditional school, to add energy and real-world relevance to an academic class?*

* *What does it mean to be a guide, and how could I transform my teaching practice to meet the needs of middle schoolers?*

* *If I want to improve my middle school, which changes should I prioritize?*

Finally, in part 4, we'll bring all of the pieces together by looking at some surprising real-life examples of what middle schoolers can do and what middle schools can be. It's time to lift our expectations. And then we'll zoom out to adult life, to remind us of why we're doing this and of what really matters during these transformative years.

But Wait — It's So Comfortable at Home

A mark of any worthwhile adventure is that we feel some reluctance to embark, some hesitation about how we might have to grow while on this path. That reluctant part of us might ask: Do I really need to change, to leave my comfortable habits? Sure, middle school was not great for me, but isn't that what we all had to go through? Or as a teacher, maybe the parts of typical middle school education that frustrate me will get better over time as my skills grow?

Well, let's consider what happens when we do middle school as usual. The typical middle school experience lies somewhere between boring and devastating, I'm sorry to say. Student ratings of school climate and connectedness to teachers, considered bellwethers of their mental health and academic success, drop significantly over the middle school years. This loss of connection is happening when kids need it most, as rates of adolescent mental health disorders skyrocket in the United States. Between 2007 and 2017, the number of US teens reporting depression increased by 59 percent overall, and faster for girls. Meanwhile, the National Institutes of Health report that nearly one in three US teens (ages thirteen to eighteen) is now expected to experience an anxiety disorder.

Even among the students who avoid such negative outcomes, the damage is often subtle but deep. Perhaps they entered middle school with enthusiasm and curiosity to learn; far too often the same child after three years has become a thoroughly passive learner, experienced at playing the game of school, checking the boxes, just waiting for the next instruction from their teacher. Their own zeal to learn was lost along the way. Or perhaps they entered as a sociable and friendly kid, and three years later find themselves lost in the popularity contest, so focused on trying to fit in and belong that they lose all sense of who they really are. Again, it does not have to be this way, but this is the all too common experience.

My own experience in middle school was in this range—I was disoriented and disconnected. School did not seem like a place to be me, or to figure out who that was. I had few friends and desperately wanted more, but had no idea how to find them. I was bored academically and figured that was just the nature of school. The only class I remember with any clarity is orchestra, where I felt somehow more creative and connected.

When I eventually went to college and cycled through various majors, trying to figure out what I wanted to do with my life, for the first few years I had one certainty: I would never do anything in education. I wanted to be far away from the routines of school and from my struggles in middle and high school. On to bigger and better things, I thought.

But life has a sense of humor to it, and as I wandered and searched for a sense of purpose, a thought began to bubble up in my mind. I knew I wanted to do something of service, to find meaning in a cause of some kind. And the thought that kept emerging was: every path leads back to education. Surely that's where the deepest changes take place? As I dusted off this taboo-to-me topic, I began to reflect differently on my own schooling. With the benefit of being a few—but not too many—years away from middle and high school, I finally asked a question that somehow had eluded me: Did it have to be so bad? I thought back to the social dislocation I felt in middle school, then to the massive achievement pressure and stress I felt in high school. Is that just what adolescence is? Or could it be different—better—even joyful?

As I write this now, twenty years have passed since I had those thoughts. And for almost all of those twenty years, I have been working with middle schoolers. First as a student teacher, where I made every mistake in the book. Then I co-founded a nonprofit called Spark and led its growth into a national organization serving thousands of middle schoolers, dedicated to reigniting their passion for learning. It was the adventure of a lifetime, ten years of working at schools across the United States. Then another adventure beckoned: the chance to start a brand-new middle school, a true lab school where we could test out ideas and reimagine the middle school experience. I jumped in with both feet, and along with our founding Board Chair and a team of extraordinary and big-thinking educators I got to help design and lead one remarkable little middle school, called Millennium School, in San Francisco.

Through these many adventures, across district-run, charter, and private schools, in cities and suburbs, in roles from teacher to principal to curriculum writer to school designer, I can sum up my lessons in a few brief thoughts. Middle schoolers are the ultimate underdogs in our world. They get so little help for the wild transformation of adolescence that they experience. They are given low expectations, told they are hormonal, and placed in learning experiences that are often out of sync with their developmental needs. But when you begin to change any of these variables, you start to see them as they truly are: engaged, curious, strange, questioning, evolving at an almost unbelievable pace. Trustworthy, respect-worthy, eager to show what they can do, ready to hold responsibility. They are on an epic adventure, one of the truly great ones in our lives. They're not children anymore. We get to witness them, like some slow-motion midair video, as they leap into adulthood. This is the promise of middle school: a magical time of discovering who you are, and what you can do, in the social world blooming around you. Let's learn how to tap into this magic.

PART 1

THE RIVER

Imagine you're rafting a whitewater river.

You twist and turn with the boat, trying not to fall out or run straight into a boulder. Water sprays your face. You paddle intensely this way and then that way. Your heart beats hard, your eyes keenly scan the river, your ears listen for what the rest of the group in your boat is saying.

Whoosh and your raft suddenly drops a few feet, a shock and a thrill at once. You're spinning now, and then you're going backward down the river, yelling out to your friends with a strange mixture of terror and excitement. *This is amazing!* And *I should never have done this.*

The water calms for a moment, and you look around at your fellow rafters. Some are laughing and some look like they're ready to crawl back into bed. They're looking at you, too, everyone trying to see if the group is OK, trying to make sense of this experience. Then without warning the boat starts to turn again, the current catches you, and you're back paddling with all your might.

If you can place yourself in this scenario, can feel the spin of the boat and that odd mixture of excitement and fear, then you have a taste of what it's like to be an adolescent. Only add in some more intensity: your body is changing, and it no longer looks or works like it did just yesterday. And your fellow rafters are not experienced navigators of the river; they are adolescents too. You're all going a little faster than seems ideal down the river. Questions loom like boulders and demand to be addressed: *Did my friend just insult me? What am I going to do when I grow up? How can I ask him out on a date?*

Adolescence is a lot like whitewater rafting. Keep this in mind when you need to generate empathy for middle schoolers. Before you react from your adult world, place yourself back in that boat. What task are they in the midst of? Where is their attention right now? When you feel the temptation to lecture them, ask yourself how helpful that is to someone in a whitewater raft, facing the intensity of the rapids, the rocks, and their fellow rafters.

We, the well-meaning adults in their lives, face our own urgent questions. *Do they even listen to me anymore? Should I intervene now or let them learn the hard way? Why are they acting like they don't want to be in our family anymore?* And perhaps most urgently: *Are they going to be OK?*

In the chapters ahead, we're going to get to know this river well. The better you know it, the less fearful you will be. You'll know when it really matters to intervene, and when it's OK if your advice is ignored. The river is our metaphor for adolescent development: the deeply engrained patterns of growth triggered by changes in the brains and bodies of young people as they mature.

Better yet: if you understand the experience of being in the raft, then you'll remember some of what it's like to be an adolescent. With understanding, it becomes easier to love them through their ups and downs, and to avoid taking things personally. If they ignore your wise words one day, it might be that a rock just appeared and they had to focus on navigating for a moment, and your comments from the shore just didn't seem relevant.

Understanding their experience on the raft lets you see beneath their behaviors. You can trace their words and actions deeper, back to their source in developmental needs and tasks. Then you know when to support them, when to challenge them, and when to simply step back.

Welcome to the river. We'll explore it carefully, examining three powerful currents (or psychological drives) as well as the course of the river and the stages of development it represents. We'll come to appreciate that development, like a river, is a powerful force. It won't help to wade into the middle of the river and command the waters to stop. You can't stop psychological development any more than you can stop your child from growing taller. Instead, we're going to learn to tap into the power of development as we help our children and students become the wise, loving, and capable people they each are. Hold on tight—we're in for an adventure.

1

WHO AM I?

As middle schoolers race down this river of development, their raft is propelled by powerful currents. Let's explore three currents in particular, in service of getting to know this river well. These three currents represent the most powerful psychological drives at play for most middle schoolers.

Each current can be thought of as a question that adolescents are driven to answer. Our job is never to answer the question for them, tempting as it may be. Rather, our task is first to know what question they're asking, and then to help create experiences that lead them to their own authentic and effective answers.

The first question is at the heart of it all: *Who am I?* To understand this, we'll journey back to Italy at the dawn of the twentieth century.

More than a century ago, an Italian physician named Maria Montessori was getting ready to break yet another barrier. Already, she had overcome stiff resistance to become the first female physician in Italy. She had been discouraged at every turn. As a medical student she was even forced to perform her required dissections of cadavers alone, after hours, because to be with her male classmates in the presence of a naked body—even a dead one—was seen as inappropriate.

But becoming the first female physician was just the beginning. Montessori became fascinated with education and wanted to apply her medical training to the way she observed children at play and at school. Thus began her revolutionary work in what was then termed "scientific pedagogy." First with mentally disabled children, then with a general population, Montessori began to study children in ways that had not been widely done before. Her findings were immediately taken up with interest by educators around the world, and today hundreds of thousands of students across thousands of schools are taught according to methods she developed in those fruitful years.

Montessori is most famous for her methods with young children, but she applied her powerful skills of observation to adolescents as well. Well before the advent of modern neuroscience, she made a claim about the essence of the middle school journey that still rings true and has since been verified amply by modern research. Her claim was this: that entering the middle school years is to be reborn, but this time into a social world. She wrote that, simply, "This is the time when the social individual is created."

The time when the social individual is created. If there were a source for our developmental river, high up in the mountains, this would be it.

Fast-forward to the current day. With the benefit of modern neuroscience and psychology, we can verify Montessori's observation. As puberty begins, most commonly during the middle school years, brain changes make young people highly sensitized to the social world. They become better at reading faces. They show stronger reactions to expressions of emotion in others. They become keenly interested in groupings, who is included and excluded, who leads and follows. They begin to track social dynamics more closely, and to wonder and experiment with how they fit into them.

Gone is the elementary school student who could effortlessly be themselves, wearing polka-dot pants or happily sharing their fascination with snails with their class. In those years, most young children are not nearly as aware of the social signals they are sending, nor of the social dynamics around them. In adolescence, they begin to see those dynamics swirling around them. This arrival into the social world can be a harsh and shocking process, like waking up to find yourself in a crowd of people talking about and looking at you.

Professor Larry Steinberg of Temple University, a leading researcher in adolescent neuroscience, describes this arrival memorably: "It's the perfect neurobiological storm, at least if you'd like to make someone painfully self-conscious: improvements in brain functioning in areas important for figuring out what other people are thinking, the heightened arousal of regions that are sensitive to social acceptance and social rejection, and the greater responsiveness to other people's emotional cues, like facial expressions."

Now take this social self-consciousness and mix in the other changes that come with puberty. Your body is changing rapidly. Your emotions are intensifying—in fact, emotional volatility peaks during the middle school years. Your mind becomes sharper, more able to think abstractly. What is the result of this heady brew? For most middle schoolers, their very identity becomes in question.

They are not sure any more if it's OK to be themselves. They notice social status and wonder if they need to copy those who have more status or more confidence. They notice what gets made fun of, and wonder if they can risk being the target of someone's laughter or taunts. On a daily basis, they face what psychologists call a choice between an *authentic self* and a *false self*. It's why the question "Who am I?" has extra charge and extra consequence for middle schoolers.

Here is where their school culture, and how we as adults relate to them, makes all the difference. If they do not feel safe psychologically—for example, because they witness bullying or intense social exclusion, or a code of values that does not allow them to explore their identity—then they are more likely to choose the path of the false self. That means copying someone else, rather than doing what is authentic to them. In copying someone else, they are trying to find social safety. The logic goes something like this: *That person seems to know what to do—they don't get bullied or teased, they seem confident—so I'll do whatever they're doing.*

The danger is, when you get stuck in a false self, you are not acting on your talents and passions, not tapping into your unique insights, sensitivities, and abilities. In trying to copy someone else, you miss your own potential.

Of course, we all go through phases of being false, maybe because we haven't realized it yet, or maybe because we're testing something out to see if it feels right. That's natural. The key is to avoid getting stuck there.

One of our central jobs then, whether as parents, teachers, mentors, or wise aunties, is to help our middle schoolers keep asking "Who am I?" and to keep wondering, in response, what is authentic to them, what feels right to them. This doesn't mean directly asking the question—more often it means inviting them into circumstances, groups, or experiences where they'll reflect on themselves in new ways and have the freedom to wonder aloud. Their job in middle school is to begin discovering who they are, and what they can do, *in a social world.* The world needs their authenticity and passion.

So, what can we do as adults to support this question? Here are some suggestions:

1. **Be yourself. Be weird.** Adolescents need to see authentic, aware adults. They need to see us be weird. Weird in this context means *honest*—not trying to pretend that every part of you fits the "normal" mold but rather embracing your quirks, eccentricities, and fascinations. We're all weird, after all—some just hide it more than others.

Even if you feel generally open with your kids or students, you may be so used to holding back certain parts of yourself that you don't even notice it anymore. See if you can catch yourself. Maybe you are afraid to show when you are upset; maybe you generously try to appear like you have it all together; maybe you don't tell them some of the more painful stories of your earlier years. Without needing to suddenly reveal everything, most of us can take one more step. One more degree of revealing, one step closer to our authentic selves. It may be the most powerful parenting and teaching we get to do.

When they see us revealing a struggle, we don't lose power—we become more honest and trustworthy. If we attempt to hide our emotions, we still give nonverbal signals, like body language or facial expressions, that reveal hints about our inner state. The result is that the words we say ("I'm fine, it's nothing") can be out of alignment with our nonverbal signals. Adolescents are quite capable of picking up this discrepancy. They may not have the insight yet to know *why* someone is hiding their feelings, but they can sense that something is off. In this uneasy place, they are less likely to feel safe and trusting.

Psychologist Mona Delahooke put it well in her book *Beyond Behaviors*, which explores the science of neuroception, or how we monitor our environment for signals of safety or threat. She wrote: "We can't hide our emotional state from a child. Emotions are transmitted from one person to the next, and through neuroception we pick up on them. Pretending to be just fine when you're really not can confuse a child and provide mixed messages about safety in relationships and how much a child can trust you to help her feel better."

We are better off revealing more, letting kids see us as highly imperfect, as we are, but also as authentic, aware, open adults. It gives them permission to be imperfect, to accept themselves, and to reveal more of their rapidly evolving inner worlds as well. They need other people to help them make sense of what's going on inside—as do we.

2. **Don't stress about self-centeredness.** It's natural to be more self-focused in times of rapid personal change. If you can imagine waking up each day with your body feeling different, your mind making leaps, your emotions intensifying, and your friendships evolving in strange and unexpected ways, then you, too, would find it natural to constantly be thinking about yourself and who you're becoming. This inward focus does *not* mean adolescents will grow into narcissistic adults.

   In fact, their self-fascination can be the beginning of a positive, perhaps lifelong, practice of self-reflection. For this reason, a well-timed gift of a journal or diary can be magical for middle schoolers. If you have personal journals or other artifacts from your adolescence, it may be time to pull them out, if only to appreciate your own self-curiosity at this age.

3. **Remember that in adolescence, identity formation is a social process.** We need other people to help us see ourselves clearly. Middle schoolers can't figure out their identity by themselves—they need varied social contexts and the experience of many different forms of influence. Ideally, they can be part of an honest and kind group of peers. This is why high-quality advisory programs, whether in or out of school, are one of the single best experiences you can offer an adolescent. One way or another, finding them a safe social space, in which they can speak honestly without fear

of being shamed, lectured, or made fun of, where they are around peers as well as open-minded adults, is of tremendous value.

4. **Encourage freedom of identity.** Middle schoolers are almost certain to experiment with their identity, often in dramatic and rapidly changing ways. They may want a new nickname or a different haircut. They may try a whole new persona among peers, complete with different language or slang. They may question their gender and sexuality, sometimes by trying on other forms of expression.

   We can support them by offering a warm, accepting, nonreactive response to their identity experiments. Be careful not to make fun of, even in ways that seem lighthearted to you, the sudden shifts they may make in identity. At the same time, don't assume that today's identity experiment will last for years. The more freedom they have to try on identities, without adults panicking or overly celebrating them, the more likely they are to find the ones that fit them best. Remember that finding their authentic self is the ticket to their most skillful, distinct, and effective ways of being in the world.

When we apply these approaches with a middle schooler, we should not expect that they'll suddenly or definitively figure out who they are. Even with the best support, it's going to be a messy process. That's natural. Adolescence is one part archaeological dig, one part busy construction site. Frequent experiments with identity, deep existential questions, and shifts in social dynamics are to be expected. The suggestions above help to give them good models of healthy adulthood, as well as the space to process and figure things out both within themselves and with their peers.

An interesting quirk of adolescence is that these years will likely be remembered better than any other phase of life. There is research, for example, that lifelong musical tastes are often formed at this age. Possibly this comes from the intensity of their emotional lives, since strong emotions help to encode experiences into our long-term memories. So the moments in which part of their identity seems to "click" and become familiar, part of their story, are moments that will last in their memory. All the more reason that it's important to access their authentic selves, to discover as openly as possible who they are.

—————————— CHAPTER SUMMARY ——————————

* Middle school is a time of social awakening, driven by brain changes that make adolescents far more sensitive to the social dynamics around them.

* As they become hyperaware of social dynamics, they have to recreate their identity, figuring out who they are and what they can do in this socially driven world.

* This can lead to a fork in the road, between creating a *false self*—for example, by copying someone cool—or creating an *authentic self*, discovering and experimenting with identities that feel right to them. The path of the authentic self is the way to tap into their fullest potential.

* We can't tell them what that authentic self is, but we can help them in other very important ways—first and foremost by revealing our own authentic selves, being more honest and open with them. We also help by accepting the natural tendencies they have at this age, like a curiosity about themselves that can seem self-centered but is quite natural at a time of rapid (and uncontrolled) personal change.

* Knowing that identity is formed socially, we can make time for their social lives and should pay attention to what peer influences are around them. And, finally, we can help establish freedom of identity, with a warm, nonreactive acceptance of the different identities they try on, sometimes in rapid succession.

For Reflection

Think back to your middle school years. What identities did you try on, or want to try on? Who in your life then seemed to represent these different possible identities or interests? How did you go about deciding what was authentically you?

_____

HOW DO I CONNECT?

Adolescence is the most peer-motivated time in life, bar none. This is the second current on our adventurous and sometimes terrifying river: the social drive. It propels middle schoolers to ask, *How do I connect?* The social drive points them away from family and toward peers, with a deep yearning to learn everything they can about friendship, groups, conflict, and more. As with all currents in this river, there is no point trying to wade in and tell it to stop. There's no way to convince them to be less interested in their peers. Instead, we can work with this current, helping them meet their social needs while including some of our goals and hopes as adults.

In the last chapter, we explored how brain changes make middle schoolers hyperaware of social dynamics, leading them to question who they are and who they "should" be. Development causes leaps to happen in their skills of social *perception,* while their skills of accurate *interpretation* lag behind. Social perception comes from brain changes and arrives whether they feel ready or not. Social interpretation comes from experience. It develops gradually through real-life trial and error.

This process of learning how to interpret social situations generates profound curiosity, often accompanied by intense confusion.

Urgent questions emerge, like *How exactly do friendships work? What make a good one? How do I get accepted by a group? Is it possible to be a member of multiple groups? What do I do when I have a crush on someone?*

This crash course in social skills is closely related to their questions about identity. *Who am I when I'm around this group? Who am I with my parents? Can I be this way with my theater friends and this other way with my soccer team? Am I willing to be the way this group wants me to be?*

Here's the catch: as well-meaning adults watching their sometimes-flailing social efforts, we can't give them the answers. We can model healthy social relationships, and that matters. And, what might be of most use, we can help them find peer groups, teams, clubs, or other social situations where they can discover parts of themselves. In fact, this will be one of the best forms of influence we have during the middle school years. But first let's take a tour through some of the major neurological and psychological factors at play.

The Peer Effect

Let's return to the work of Larry Steinberg, professor at Temple University and a leading expert on adolescent development. He and colleagues conducted a series of fascinating studies on risk-taking in adolescence. They came to an intriguing conclusion: while the popular story often blames peer pressure to explain adolescent recklessness, a bigger cause is actually the pleasure youth take in each other's company, and how that primes their brains to look for more pleasure.

In neuroscience terms, this is called *reward priming*, which means that when we experience one form of "reward" or pleasure, it tends to increase (or "prime") our desire to experience more. Think of a time when you were having such a wonderful time with a friend that you felt motivated to splurge on some ice cream and enjoy that together. The reward of good company primed you to gain even more pleasure from another reward, in this case ice cream. For adolescents, whose brains are particularly motivated by their social drive, this effect means that simply being around peers is a hugely rewarding, pleasurable experience. They turn further toward peers because of how much enjoyment it provides, not because they hate adults.

Steinberg and his colleagues coined a term for this phenomenon: the *peer effect*. Keep this in mind as you witness your child or student become increasingly oriented to the peer world. They are not doing this to spite you but rather because their evolving brains make it a highly rewarding activity. If they deeply want to hang out with friends, it may not be the right move to let them skip family dinner, but you can understand where they're coming from. If they seem to struggle greatly to focus in a traditional class format because they want to connect with friends, it is not necessarily because of a lack of respect for the teacher but perhaps just the extremely rewarding peer experience also on offer to them. This is their time to learn how to be among peers. After all, for most of their lives, that's who will matter most.

Becoming an Individual

This turn toward peers is often a painful process for parents. The child you knew, the way they looked up to you (even if there was also conflict), and the relative simplicity of their world are all changing almost beyond recognition. In their place is a proto-adult, who aims to look at you from a more eye-to-eye perspective (and perhaps physically eye-to-eye now as well), immersed in a complex social world into which you can't fully see. You may sense that your influence over them is waning. It's normal for parents to feel a sense of grief as they witness their child shifting away from family and home as their center, and toward peers instead.

If it's any solace, remember that this process is absolutely normal and healthy. It is a developmental phase that means a child is beginning their transition into adulthood. Yes, it often begins an arc that will take them away from you in the short term, but when you support them well, it means they will come back to you as adults, ready to engage and become something closer to friends.

There is a word for this process: *individuation.* It means, simply, the process of becoming an individual, distinct from one's family of origin. For adolescents, brain development calls them toward the world of their peers, to discover who they are and find their place among others. It's as though adults are coming through in black-and-white, their words in subtitles, while peers are in full, living, vibrant color and sound. There's no competition in any contest for attention.

The task for parents, then, is to respect that individuation is developmentally normal and inevitable, even if it is painful at times. If we assume that it's driven by brain changes, we can take it less personally. We can see it coming, avoid resisting it when it does, and instead of fighting to keep our kids closer than they want to be, we can prepare them for this change and put our energy into guiding them toward new social situations.

How might this look in practice? My wife tells a story about her childhood that has always stuck with me. Sometime in her elementary school years, she remembers sitting down with her father and hearing something surprising. He told her that, while it might seem crazy to her now, there would soon come a time when she would think he and her mother were annoying and embarrassing, even stupid. She remembers being shocked and telling her father not to worry, that she would never think that.

Some years later and well into puberty, she indeed arrived at the point of being aggravated and embarrassed by her parents. But she remembered that her parents had predicted this and, in a strange way, that proved they weren't actually stupid. While she had the normal tween and teen frustrations, this conversation smoothed the road a little. Her parents had demonstrated that they understood something important about her development, were not going to fight it, and were even preparing her for it.

New Ways to Be Influential

Seeing a child enter this individuation process does not mean we have to give up on being influential. Far from it. But we have to find new ways. As they turn toward peers, we can turn with them. We'll find new forms of influence, and will be of genuine service, by helping them find groups they love being in. This is not a "nice to have"—it's essential developmentally. Middle schoolers discover who they are through others. It's what their brains are primed for.

To understand why peer relationships shape who we become, consider that being with peers activates far more powerful learning than, say, a typical academic experience. Immersion in a new peer group activates our powers of adaptation, which might just be the most under-appreciated human talent.

Say you're a middle schooler who has just joined a group, like a soccer team or a new lunch table. Now you're picking up social signals, language, mindsets, values, skills, and new ways of relating. In fact, you're not just picking these up—as you spend time swimming in these new ways of being, you're becoming more like the group. You're adapting.

Day by day, your words will shift. Your way of seeing the world will evolve. Even your body language will become more like that of the others. This is why adaptation is a superpower: on more levels than our conscious minds can even make sense of, we absorb the behaviors of the people around us. It's why it's so important to find groups whose values align with your authentic self, and to have the freedom to change groups and identities as you discover who you are.

So how do we support this social drive, and how do we remain influential as peers become the focus? Here are some suggestions:

1. **Make space and time for their social drive.** Remember that this time in life is an ideal opportunity to build social intelligence, perhaps the best, because adolescents' brains are so socially oriented. If they're busy all day in highly structured activities, or in classes where they mainly interact with the teacher, then they won't get the practice they need to develop their social intelligence, and they'll almost certainly be frustrated about it. Instead, make sure they have ample time, ideally every day, to be around peers.

2. **Provide help when needed.** If they are struggling consistently to find their people, we can provide some help, provided we use a light touch. Doing the work for them for any extended period of time is not helpful and could actually slow down their social learning. But if they are stuck, lonely, or frustrated about their lack of friendships, then we may be able to help.

   This might mean directly inviting them to try a new group or activity. Better yet, find informal, indirect ways to help them discover new groups. It might mean arranging a carpool, walk, or public-transit ride to school with peers, offering a bit of regular, casual social time. Or noticing that they look up to a certain peer, and asking that peer to invite people to try out for an activity they do, from a theater production to a debate club. It might mean creating a light bit of structure, within which a middle schooler has choice, to prompt an experiment—like framing the beginning of the school year as a time for everyone to sign up for at least one club or team, but giving them the choice of which one.

   In all of these cases, the middle schoolers still have to do the hard work. They're the ones on the developmental crash course in social skills. Our job is to help create the conditions for them to explore and discover parts of their identity among others.

3. **Encourage membership in multiple groups with different values.** One of the most helpful challenges we can offer a middle schooler is to be a member of multiple groups who value different things. If they first find their community among the basketball team, beautiful; but if they can also learn how to thrive in an improv group, or among neighborhood friends who don't care about basketball, they'll be even better off. Adolescents benefit by seeing that they can bring different parts of themselves out among different people. It helps them experiment with identity and develop the ever-useful skill of code switching, in which we learn how to adapt our language, tone, and behavior to connect with people.

   These experiences also protect adolescents from getting stuck in conformity. While it's developmentally natural to go through a conformity phase, during which they may want to be identical to a best friend or small circle of friends, we want to make sure they aren't stuck in this stage for too long. Learning to connect with different groups, adapting yourself and finding success in different ways, leads them beyond conformity.

4. **Use the power of the "third thing."** Most adolescents enjoy the experience of being side-by-side with peers while looking at something or someone else, like a movie, a social situation, a game, or a funny YouTube clip. This is the third thing beyond the two (or more) peers. Having a third thing to look at and comment on gives them a break from face-to-face connection, which can engage their social brain so intensely that it can be exhausting or anxiety-producing.

It often invites them to speak more openly. Many parents have discovered the secret of driving with their child, in which a conversation that is not face-to-face can be surprisingly deep and honest. If a middle schooler is having trouble connecting with peers, you can use the power of the third thing by finding ways for them to make friends over a shared interest or hobby. Working side-by-side to build a model airplane, complete a puzzle, or make a funny video together might be an ideal way for a friendship to form or deepen.

5. **Accept social conflict as natural, normal, and an ideal learning opportunity.** Middle schoolers are making leaps in their social insights and in the way they can use words to connect with (or attack) others. Sometimes it's like someone handed them a sword ten times too big and heavy for them, and while they try to wield it with grace, they might accidentally lop off someone's arm or chop a wall in half without meaning to. In other words, all their new social skills take time to become practiced and thoughtfully used, and in the meantime, they're likely to make mistakes and find themselves in conflict.

As the adults in their lives, our first job is to not make conflicts worse, which we could do by adding our own anger, blaming them, or seeking punishment before we get to the bottom of things. Instead, we can use conflict as an ideal learning opportunity. After all, we learn best when new information is paired with emotion and relationship. So it follows that the tools you offer in conflict, which is going to be socially and emotionally charged, are likely to be remembered. Approaches like Restorative Justice or Nonviolent Communication offer ways to resolve conflicts and learn sophisticated social and emotional skills in the process.

6. **Find a facilitated peer group to help adolescents process their social experiences.** Knowing that at some point they will become less keen to seek advice from adult authority figures, the question becomes, Where else will they get it from? The defaults would likely be peers or the internet, both of which can provide useful advice but are equally likely to provide problematic suggestions or simply not respond in ways that a young person needs in the moment. These sources will be in play anyway, but if you have the opportunity, you can help them by finding a *facilitated peer group* experience. This can be through an advisory program at school, a youth mentorship program, a scouting program, faith groups, or after-school advisory programs (see chapter 14). Wherever you find this, the key is a group of similar-age peers (say, middle school only, or sometimes age or grade specific), led by a trusted adult who is not grading or lecturing them but rather keeps the space safe for honest conversation.

CHAPTER SUMMARY

* The social drive is paramount at this age. Don't try to stop it, but rather work with it as a new way to have influence.

* Imagine how good it feels to see an old, dear friend for a heart-to-heart conversation. It feels *at least* that good for your student or child to spend time with their friends, given the social sensitivity of the adolescent brain. If we take to heart how immensely appealing peers are, knowing that this is the direct result of brain changes, we'll understand middle schoolers much better.

* *Individuation* means that adolescents will seek some separation from their family, in more or less graceful ways. Peers will be on

center stage. It can be painful, but this process is healthy. If you can prepare for it and help them anticipate it, trusting it as a phase rather than a mentality they'll hold forever, you may have a smoother passage through.

* Your ability to help them find positive peers and groups to be with is one of the most powerful forms of influence you have at this age.

* We can help middle schoolers complete their developmental tasks by offering substantial time for socializing, even during the school day. Better yet, when they socially connect with various groups whose values are different, they discover more of themselves and learn to adapt. Being a member of a facilitated peer group is also a powerful resource, offering them space to make sense of their social and identity questions.

* Social conflict is normal at this age—it's how we respond to it that ultimately makes it a harmful or helpful experience. Seize the teachable moment that conflict presents to deepen social-emotional skills.

For Reflection

What do you remember about your social life in middle school? How did it evolve? Beyond your parents, who were your primary influences at this age?

WHAT WILL I CONTRIBUTE?

On a bright spring day nearly 100 people, mostly students, streamed out of a middle school carrying signs in protest of the school shootings that seemed to be happening more and more often. The students were angry, passionate, determined, and also curious to see what would happen when they began to speak out, to demand that politicians make changes to prevent these massacres. They walked onto the street tentatively, casting side glances at each other, singing their protest song a little quietly. Then the honking began.

At first it wasn't clear if the car horns were a good sign, but then the students saw the drivers cheering and rolling down their windows to yell their support. Everyone marched with a little more pep and vigor as the busy city street around them came alive with honks and cheers. Their singing got louder. Passersby started pulling out their phones to film and photograph and post news of the march on social media, and soon it was shared around the city. People came out of storefronts to watch the students and clap as they passed by.

This one group of middle schoolers, who had spent the evening before making signs and T-shirts, were having their voices heard. People watched them on social media and on the TV news, and knew that a group of young people had said something important. It didn't mean change happened instantly, but it was an important contribution, and a training for students who had decades ahead of them to be active citizens.

I was a proud principal witnessing my students in this moment, watching as they marched on. They had surprised themselves. They were making a memory of speaking and being heard, on an important topic, and the real-world proof was in the authentic reactions of total strangers.

How to Feel Valuable

How do we realize that we have something valuable to contribute? Or to take it deeper: How do we realize that we *are* a valuable contribution to the world?

Simply put: we feel valuable by doing things of value for others. Adolescents, whose identity is formed through social connection, need to see the value they offer reflected in the eyes of others. They need to see others look at them a little differently, recognizing their capability and that they have used it well.

Let's return for a moment to Maria Montessori and her wise perspective on adolescents. While it is not widely known outside of Montessori education, she made a quite extraordinary recommendation for what middle schools should be. Her suggestion was that middle schoolers should live on and operate a farm and inn. They would be required to constantly work together to create value for others, through the food they grew and the service they offered to customers at the inn. It may not be a practical idea to take to scale, but as a north star, it points us directly toward what middle schoolers need to thrive. After even a year in such an environment, it's easy to imagine that they would feel confident in their abilities to contribute work of value to both peers and the wider world.

Whether working on a farm or not, as adolescents mature into adults, they can internalize this sense of value. They can become their own judge of their efforts, even when something important they do may not be appreciated by others. But they first need to see the effect they have on others. That is why that protest march was so powerful for the students involved: they heard in the cheers and honks of strangers that they were saying something important, and they began to internalize the belief that they had important things to say.

This is the third current in our river, the deep drive of adolescents to answer the question: *What will I contribute?* It's a question they might hold in a group project, on a sports team, in a friend group, or in relation to the adult life they see barreling toward them. When they have chances to answer this question, to discover their ability through experience, they gain a deep-seated confidence, a look-you-in-the-eyes sense of personal dignity.

To discover how to help them answer this question, we have to begin with ourselves. Let's explore a bias that most adults carry, one that creates no end of conflict and frustration with the adolescents in our lives.

The Anchoring Effect

Adolescents are aware of their rapidly growing capabilities in the world. Yes, they may overestimate themselves—but they are all too familiar with adults underestimating them. The gap between these two views leads to much of the frustration between adolescents and adults.

To understand and get beyond this tension, it helps to understand the *anchoring effect*. It's a simple but powerful and well-documented bias in human perception. It means that information we receive first (about someone or something) tends to "anchor" us and is given more significance than later information. This effect explains the classic advice about why first impressions matter; even if we revise our opinion of someone, it is often *relative* to how we first saw them. We remember that first experience more, and it has outsized influence on our later decisions.

This means that for someone as rapidly changing as an adolescent, we are almost certainly lagging behind them in our sense of what they're ready for. As a mentor of mine put it, you may find yourself cutting their pancakes when they already know how to make the batter. As a parent, looking at the twelve-year-old in front of you, your reasoning may be anchored by memories of them as a small child. That child who was so recently (it seems) three years old and liable to run into traffic—how can they be capable of taking the subway on their own now? We're anchored on past experiences of them and likely missing some of what is right in front of us.

For teachers, too, if you've seen a student in past years or heard about them from colleagues in lower grades, you may be anchoring on old information. Even if you have them for one year of middle school, the person they were in September might be quite different from how they show up in April.

The anchoring effect leads us to inadvertently talk down to adolescents, to see them as less capable than they are, and to give them less freedom and responsibility as a result. Is there anything that annoys them more?

So the question is: How can we correct this anchoring effect bias by offering them more responsibility and freedom at home or at school? If we accept that we are likely underestimating them, what would we do differently?

Keep in mind that middle school students show a wide range of maturity, and in the space of an hour they can be capable of both deep introspection and the grossest potty humor. But like all of us, they want to be given the respect associated with the high end of their personal range of maturity. One way we do this is by honoring their ability to contribute.

The key here is that we adults need to position ourselves more as bridges to the world, and less as walls to protect them from it. This doesn't mean suddenly releasing them into the wilderness of the internet or your nearest city. Rather, it means gradually pushing your comfort zone. Instead of getting caught up in fear about the "real world" and how it might chew up the young people we love, remind yourself that they are already seeing and experiencing more of it than we realize, and they need to learn how to interact with it. As with anything, that learning comes best through actual experience.

What does this mean in practice? Here are some suggestions:

1. **Middle schoolers need meaningful work.** To feel valuable, they need to do things of value for others. Working for their school community, for their family, or in paid jobs when old enough are all routes toward this. The key is that the work has evident value. The same chores they've had since elementary school may feel too childish. What can they do now that they could not do before?

    Schoolwork *can* count as meaningful work, but the truth is that it rarely does. If middle schoolers see their schoolwork as something contrived, for which only their (subjective) teacher is the audience, it is not likely to carry the weight of real-world contribution. It is possible to make schoolwork feel meaningful enough to meet this need, however. We'll explore this more in chapter 17.

2. **Middle schoolers need time with objective adults.** The older an adolescent gets, the more they will measure them-selves against the adult world. Whether they're eager to leap into adulthood or are all-out resisting it, they know it's coming. This excitement and anxiety about the world is a ready source of motivation if we know how to tap into it by using the power of relevance.

When we ask an adolescent to do something, whether for their family or within an academic project, it's on us to make it clear that this task is relevant. Often, the surest route is to show them that "real" adults—in other words, those who are objective, not highly subjective like parents and teachers—do this task or struggle with the problem it represents.

Perhaps the best example of this, described more in part 3, is the use of outside experts to judge their work. If they're doing a writing project, for example, let their final grade come at least in part from a few volunteers who are professional writers, editors, or publishers. The effect on their motivation, compared to providing something to a teacher whose whims they know, is dramatic. They will surprise themselves with their abilities through the challenge of coming face-to-face with an objective adult. They'll also take the results more seriously, and when they do well will feel they have done something important.

3. **Give their opinions power—even complaints.** At every opportunity, consider if you can offer them a choice. Even if it is a choice between options you have preselected. Consider also if you can give them greater voice in the events of their lives, shifting from passive childlike roles to a more active role, for example, by turning parent-teacher conferences into student-led conferences in which they guide the entire conversation.

One of the best signals here is the frequency and nature of their complaints. Complaining is often a way of making a claim on adult reasoning. Consciously or not, many complaints come from the desire to show that they have their own opinions, that they can decide for themselves what is good and bad, and that they can speak up. If their complaining is frequent, it may be a request to be taken more seriously. They may be saying they're ready for more control over choices in their lives.

4. **Don't ignore the charged topics of the day.** It's understandable to worry that the latest scandal or dire news is more than they can handle, particularly when we witness emotional volatility over what may seem to us like relatively small matters. Here again, though, we may be making a mistake and protecting them in a way that does not ultimately help them grow. After all, if a topic of the day is truly charged, that means it is full of energy and relevance. Chances are, middle schoolers are more aware of what is going on in the world than you may realize, as the keen observers they are. Yet they may have perception without accurate interpretation. Our task is to help them make sense of the world by relating to it, not shielding them from it. We can bring up these charged topics, help them understand the nuance (and avoid falling into black-and-white, "our side is right and the other side is crazy" thinking), and for teachers even use these topics as an invitation into engaging academic studies. Why pass up a ready source of motivation and interest in the world?

Ultimately, we want adolescents to witness themselves doing things of value for others, and so to internalize a sense of their own value and self-worth. When a middle schooler has had these experiences, receiving the trust of adults and believing their work has relevance, the effect is palpable. They take themselves more seriously and will show us more of the real potential of this age.

---------------------------- CHAPTER SUMMARY ----------------------------

* Middle schoolers feel valuable by doing things of value for others. When they see they have made a contribution, they internalize the belief that they can contribute positively.

* The *anchoring effect* explains how adults tend to let their earlier impressions of young people guide them, and thus are often slow to realize how capable or ready an adolescent is for more responsibility. This is a primary source of frustration for adolescents, who want their growing capabilities to be appreciated and trusted by the adults around them.

* We can help middle schoolers by offering them meaningful work, from more complex chores at home or school to paid work. We can also listen differently to their complaints, receiving them as signals that they can take on more responsibility or would like their opinion to be taken more seriously.

* Our key task is to become bridges to the real world, facilitators of interactions with it, rather than instructors about it. How can we help them have experiences in which they feel real limits in the world, interact with objective adults who are not beholden to them in any way, and in which they are challenged to make a contribution?

For Reflection

Think of a time when you suddenly gained new responsibility as an adolescent, like your first part-time job. How did it affect you? If you never had this kind of experience, what kind of trust or responsibility do you wish you had been given?

DEVELOPMENTAL STAGES

We've explored the currents in this river of development, always pushing middle schoolers to wonder who they are, how to connect with others, and how to feel valuable in a widening world. With luck, this understanding has offered you new ways to support them on their adventure. But now that we know how the river flows, a new question emerges: Where is the river taking us?

To answer this question, we need to understand the stages of development that most adolescents go through, like the twists and turns of a river. If the adventure begins with the rapid brain changes caused by puberty, it then travels through three primary stages—Belonging, Achievement, and Authenticity—each defined by distinct motivations and offering new abilities to think and relate. There are clear markers for each stage, and we can use these to orient ourselves to what an adolescent needs from us right now.

At heart, each stage brings an adolescent new abilities to see and handle complexity. An early middle schooler, for example, might at first use concrete, black-and-white thinking. When the teacher explains a rule, they accept it as fact. They might accept specific roles given them (like what boys are "supposed" to do or be like), and they might prefer academics that use tangible or visible examples rather than abstractions. But by the end of middle school, having grown into new stages, this same middle schooler will be a far more complex thinker. They'll be able to see shades of gray in the rules they're told. They may question authority and draw their own conclusions. They'll perceive nuance in social relations and can appreciate that the roles we play may depend on where we are or who we're with. Year by year, in leaps and stumbles, they become more complex.

Over the years, many theories have emerged to explain how humans develop this more complex thinking. The Swiss psychologist Jean Piaget is famous in the education world for the stages of development he proposed, which offer an explanation for how young people shift from concrete to more abstract forms of thinking. Abraham Maslow theorized a "hierarchy of needs," commonly shown as a pyramid, which we climb up as we progress. It begins with our basic needs for water, food, and sleep, then progresses to safety needs, then learning how to secure love and belonging, finding esteem, and finally striving for self-actualization, which activates our full potential as humans. This, too, is a developmental theory, showing how we go from simpler needs to something as complex and abstract as self-actualization. Many others have added important theories since Maslow and Piaget's time, from Jenny Wade's holonomic theory to Michael Commons's model of hierarchical complexity. For more on these, take a look at Appendix 1: Developmental Research.

Why is all of this important? You don't need to become an expert on developmental theory, but you *do* need to understand what human potential looks like during the very unique time that is middle school. This is what we'll explore in the next three chapters. If we don't have a clear-eyed view of human abilities at this age, we'll end up using less helpful measures. *What is the neighbor's kid doing? How are your standardized test scores?* These are poor measures of whether a middle schooler is reaching their potential. We need a deeper way to know how someone is evolving. That way is understanding what stage of development they are in.

From Piaget to Commons, many have proposed their own theories of human development; there is not yet any clear, agreed-upon approach to unite these or identify one that is most accurate. However, by integrating the major models of human development, and focusing on the early adolescent years, a clear pattern emerges. Across eight different theorists' and researchers' work, three stages appear again and again in the adolescent years. They offer us a deeper way to understand what we're really working toward and hoping for during this transformative age.

Enough Theory—Let's Make It Personal

To understand these stages, imagine yourself in the following story. If possible, read this slowly and notice the feelings, images, or sensations that emerge. The empathy you generate here will help you be of greatest service to the middle schoolers in your care.

Imagine that you have just made a remarkable leap of faith. For reasons you can hardly explain, you decided to leave your job and your country of origin. You're going to move to a foreign country and take on a job you have never done before. It's not even in the same field of work as your past experience.

Today is your first day in your new job. Everything is new: the people, the clothing, the language, the type of work you're expected to do, the social rules. You walk in wide-eyed. You feel fear, curiosity, and the sheer newness of the experience.

What might be going through your mind in a situation like this? It's likely you would be asking yourself, "Did I make the right decision to come here? Am I welcome? Is this the right place for me?" As you learn people's names, discover the rules, and try to figure out what is expected of you, you'll be wondering all the while if you belong.

If you get the sense that you don't belong—people shun you, the work is strange and beyond your understanding, your efforts are met with unfriendly responses—then it would be natural to panic. Maybe you've made a terrible mistake. Full of anxiety and fear, you may wonder if you should even try to succeed. This is what happens when our core sense of belonging is threatened. But let's say that things proceed more positively.

As your first days go by, you notice little positive signals. Your co-workers invite you to lunch and take time to chat with you. You are picking up the language quickly. A few people are particularly kind, going out of their way to explain the rules and help you settle in. Your first friendships begin to emerge. You start to feel welcome, like you belong. Your nervous system seems to relax, as you feel greater familiarity and less potential threat. You begin to gain some faith that eventually, with help, you will learn what you need to.

You are meeting the need to belong, the fundamental task of this first stage. As your confidence grows, you no longer ask yourself if you should be here or if success is possible. It feels within reach, with effort and help. You are beginning to tap into your motivation to achieve. Whatever your new friends and colleagues see as excellence, you would like to have it, to earn it. It would feel so good to see that they respect your skills and efforts. This is the second phase, characterized by the desire to achieve.

Years have now gone by. From a raw beginning, without friends or skills in the job, you've found both. You have several trusted friends and are part of several groups. You've begun to excel in your job. Your colleagues and superiors are impressed with you, not just for your effort but for the actual product of your work. Promotions and official recognition come your way. You begin to internalize the feeling that you're skillful, that you have what it takes.

Now something else is dawning in you. As you feel more and more confident in this particular job, more secure in the praise and promotions you've received, you begin to wonder: What is it that I love to do? Why do

I feel more inspired and connected to certain activities, less so to others? What am I uniquely good at here?

You begin to change. Building on your security in belonging, and your confidence as a capable member of the community, you begin to tinker. What if I focused on this particular part of the job? What if I did my job more artistically? What if I spent more time exploring this passion? You begin to want to help others do the same. You're not sure if you care about the next promotion as much as getting to explore this passion of yours.

You are entering the phase of authenticity, in which you have gained the ability to belong and to achieve, but you no longer want to achieve just to win someone else's game. You want to bring things to the world that are unique to you, that draw out both heart and mind.

You have just completed a developmental journey. You've sought belonging, then achievement, then authenticity. In life we may repeat this three-stage cycle in new relationships, in new jobs, and especially—the most intense version of all—in adolescence.

We'll explore each stage, what it looks like in the daily life of a middle schooler, how to help young people meet their developmental tasks, and when to challenge them on to further growth.

Before we dive into the first stage, Belonging, there are a few general principles to keep in mind when thinking about these developmental stages.

First: don't confuse the map for the territory. Developmental stage models are extremely helpful for certain things, but any one person is far too complex to be labeled with one single stage that represents them entirely. Rather, you can see a stage as the place they're most likely to be found right now.

Second: development is not a one-way journey. As adults, we may go through this three-stage journey multiple times. We may even be going through multiple versions of it at the same time. Perhaps we're finding our way in a new friend group, tentatively seeking belonging, but feel highly skillful and authentic in our work life.

Third: while the sequence of development tends to be consistent, the pace varies tremendously. In middle school, a new sixth grader might be more mature than a seventh grader. And that young-seeming seventh grader might make a huge leap in the span of a few months. In cases of trauma, someone may actually move backward in the sequence, returning to earlier stages of development as they pursue essential needs for security. So you can't expect a middle schooler to proceed at a regular speed or really at any preplanned pace at all. The key is to observe and facilitate rather than try to direct their development.

Our first task, as the adults supporting a middle schooler, is to locate them developmentally. When we know where they are, we know what their tasks are. Then we can position ourselves to help them complete those tasks. This keeps their development progressing, keeps their motivation strong, and aligns our goals with theirs, so they see us as helpful companions rather than adults dragging them in a direction they don't want to go.

Let's begin where they begin: with the essential stage of finding *belonging*.

—————————— CHAPTER SUMMARY ——————————

* After we understand the developmental drives of middle schoolers, which are like the currents propelling them down a river, the next question is: Where is the river taking us? There are three distinct stages of this river, representing three developmental stages that most middle schoolers will experience.

* These three stages, each defined by their core motivation, are Belonging, Achievement, and Authenticity.

* These stages tend to go in order, with middle schoolers seeking belonging first, then wanting to achieve and find excellence in

some regard, and finally beginning to bring more of their personal authenticity and passions to light among others.

* We can apply this concept to help locate a child by determining which stage they're likely experiencing. When we know where they are, we know which developmental task they're facing. Then we can help create the conditions for them to complete those tasks and continue growing.

For Reflection

Can you think of a time when you made a leap between stages in your life? For example, a time when you finally felt you belonged— or a time when you wanted to bring more of yourself to a role and cared less about achieving what you were traditionally "supposed" to achieve?

BELONGING

We need belonging almost as badly as we need water. We feel the need for belonging as though our lives depend on it—which should be no surprise, because for much of our evolutionary history, they did. Our species evolved in groups, survived by belonging to groups, and even in our modern and more individualistic society, is still wired to seek belonging as one of our deepest needs.

As adults, our life experience helps us handle dry spells in our sense of belonging. We may be able to draw on past memories of connection or community and trust we'll find it again. We can use the resources, freedom of movement, and mental tools we've accumulated to remind ourselves that we do belong or to find belonging if we need it, say by making time to visit family or old friends.

But for adolescents, immersed in the intense world of peers, social brains newly activated, and without the benefit of years of adult experience, feeling they belong is an urgent need now. Even one incident of not belonging—like getting the cold shoulder from a friend at lunchtime—can be devastating. In their eyes that cold shoulder means the loss of a friendship, often for confusing or unclear reasons. The prospect of wandering the cafeteria or halls without a place to be or people who will welcome you is terrifying.

Until their sense of belonging is secure, middle schoolers will not reach anything close to their full potential. Without belonging, most won't feel safe enough to bring out their gifts, to experiment with their identity to find what is authentic to them, or to take the risks and apply the energy needed to reach their academic potential. That's why belonging is the beginning of any good journey through middle school. It's the first stage of this river of adolescence we're rafting.

Unfortunately, many middle schools are not set up to help students find belonging. In a traditional middle school, particularly a large one, even the best-intentioned adults may have minimal time for anything beyond academic instruction. Noticing if a student has few friends or is getting socially isolated, and having the time to intervene and do something about it, is often seen as a luxury. Perhaps this is why the research shows that students' sense of belonging falls during middle school, as does the related sense of connectedness to school.

Here's the good news, though: once we acknowledge belonging as primary, we can get to work with known tools and help make it happen. The first step is to recognize the signals that a child is working on the tasks of the Belonging stage. Keep an eye out for behaviors like these below, which tell you that their current and most important developmental task is to find people to belong with:

1. **"Best friends forever."** This phrase, or others like it, often signals that the quest for belonging has come to focus on one or two very close friends. They may seem to want to "twin" or become nearly identical, with similar clothing, hobbies, attitudes, language, and more.

2. **Conformity.** The quest for belonging often leads to conformity, whether with a best friend, a group, or a popular style. This can be painful for adults to witness, but unless someone is being harmed, some conformity is developmentally normal and does not require intervention. A phase of

conformity is often a natural side effect of seeking belonging; we only need to worry if they seem to be stuck in it for years, which we'll explore later.

3. **The membership self.** You may detect a sense of do-or-die membership—a deep fear that if a friendship goes away or a group rejects them, they will have nothing and will be totally lost or worthless. Some psychologists refer to this as "the membership self," in which self-esteem and meaning come from a person's sense of belonging to a group. It is a vulnerable and scary place to be, but it is often a normal place to pass through on their developmental journey.

4. **Concrete "role" thinking.** Cognitively, young people at this stage are often concrete, black-and-white thinkers. They might use simple reasoning when it comes to who they belong with and who they don't—like "I only hang out with girls, I hate boys" or "My friends are awesome but I don't like other humans." They tend to not be as self-aware or reflective as in later stages. They may accept group norms at face value, without question or critique. This, too, will change in time and is not cause for concern so long as it is a passing phase.

These are some of the many signals that tell you Belonging is the key developmental goal of the moment.

How Do We Support Them at This Stage?

Now that you've located your child or student developmentally, you can position yourself alongside them, helping to create the conditions for them to experience belonging. Here are some steps to consider:

1. **Make sure they have at least one peer group where they feel fully accepted.** At minimum, one friend. This before all else.

Honor that this need is much deeper and more existential than almost any other psychological need. Whether as parents or teachers, if we see a middle schooler who is consistently struggling to belong, active help may be needed.

We have to be careful not to act too early, as some fumbling around socially is normal, particularly in times of transition like the start of a new school year. But if the struggles continue, we can sensitively and tactfully begin to provide support. We might offer them a set of choices for clubs, teams, or groups and ask them to choose one, perhaps framing it as the time of year to make this choice. If there is a way to prompt a peer invitation, without creating a sense of pity or shame, that is even better. Coming from someone their age, the offer to join a group, club, team, or simply a lunch table can be a turning point.

Worry less about the scope of their social life; at first they don't need multiple groups or even many friends. But we should work to make sure they have at least one friend or group who welcomes them and enjoys their company.

2. **Appreciate that belonging may be even more important for students in marginalized groups.** When a student feels that part of their identity is marginalized or not part of the dominant narrative, they may have a greater need to form a strong group with others like them. Beverly Daniel Tatum described this effect in her book *Why Are All the Black Kids Sitting Together in the Cafeteria?*, writing that "racial grouping is a developmental process in response to an environmental stressor, racism. Joining with one's peers for support in the face of stress is a positive coping strategy." This need to belong can enable students to steep themselves in the symbols, culture, and stories of a marginalized group, strengthening this identity, and ultimately enabling more positive interaction beyond this group.

3. **Make sure they have social time in their schedule.** If we want middle schoolers to feel they belong among peers, we have to provide time for them to find the right peers, to make the natural social mistakes and recover from them, and to simply enjoy their peers' company. All of this means that the school day, after-school hours, and weekends need to incorporate ample social time.

Depending on their personality, they may prefer this to be less structured social time, like hanging out after school; those who are more introverted may prefer a more structured way to interact, perhaps in an advisory group or through a team that has a shared focus like sports or debate.

4. **Offer space to process the social bumps in the road.** If things go well, they're going to be on an adventure of finding and losing friends, gradually learning that they can create belonging. They'll need a space to process what went well and what went wrong. This could be an advisory program at school (see more in chapter 16), a youth mentoring program, Scouts or other groups, camps, etc. The ideal is a group of peers who are facilitated by an adult they trust, who makes it safe and interesting for them to speak their minds and be present for each other through the adventures of adolescence.

In such a group, it's possible to directly speak about and teach skills in areas like how to make a friend. After all, these are fundamental skills, and too often adults assume that kids will pick them up by intuition or observation alone. Some will, but many will be confused, and there's no need to leave them in that confusion. A trusted adult can facilitate conversations between middle schoolers around questions like: *How did you become friends with one of your closest friends? Have you ever had a conflict in a friendship, and what did you do to repair it? Did it work? Have you ever been rejected by a group, and how did you deal with it?* These conversations may be some of the most relevant and useful during this age.

How Do We Challenge a Middle Schooler to Go Beyond This Stage?

Our first goal is always to help them complete the developmental tasks of a given stage. If you've determined that your child or student is at the Belonging stage, that means that job #1 is to feel connected with peers, whether in a close friendship, a handful of those, or a formal or informal group.

If things go well, then at some point they will begin to grow beyond this stage. They may become tired of conformity or feel constrained by the unspoken rules of a friendship or group. They may begin to realize that they can be part of multiple groups or even that they can generate their own belonging. They'll show growing confidence in their ability to make friends.

Some young people get stuck in this stage. For reasons ranging from earlier trauma, to stressful home or school environments, to simply a different pace of maturing, they may seem to hang on to a conformist, belonging-at-all-costs mentality for years.

Whether they're proceeding on their own or seem to be stuck in this phase, our choices as adults can help set the conditions for them to move to the next stage. We can't force it to happen, but through modeling and the right experiences, we can invite them to the next stage. They'll accept the invitation when they are ready. Here are some ways to begin:

1. **Adult modeling.** Chances are, as a parent or teacher reading this, you have experienced belonging at different times and places, and you are no longer seeking it with the same do-or-die urgency as a middle schooler. You have developed a more sophisticated view of social relationships—for example, you know that you might bring out one side of yourself

in this group and another in that other group. You know that you can create belonging, not just find it, by using skills to build trust with others. You have probably faced challenges of repairing relationships, learning that ruptures do not always lead to the end of a relationship but can be fixed and even create stronger ties in the future. In short, you have the ability to model the mindsets and skills of later stages of development.

The more open you are in sharing these experiences, both from your past and when they are happening in the present, the more useful and available your knowledge is for the middle schoolers in your life.

2. **Invite them to join multiple groups with differing values.** One of the antidotes to conformity is to realize that you *want* to be in two (or more) groups, whose values are different, and who will require you to follow different rules. If you want to be part of them badly enough—say, you really enjoy hanging out with your Model United Nations team but also love your skateboarding friends—then you will be pushed to grow beyond conformity, beyond a simple black-and-white view of what is correct and incorrect behavior. As adults, we can help adolescents experience this, if they seem stuck in just one group, by finding ways for them to be invited into different groups or experience different cultures. The ideal route is to facilitate an invitation from a peer, rather than from an authority figure.

3. **Self-reflection practices.** One of the extraordinary cognitive leaps in adolescence is toward *metacognition*—the ability to step back and look at yourself and your thinking. The beginnings of this skill often can be seen at younger ages, but growth in metacognition accelerates dramatically in adolescence. This is why self-reflection practices, like

keeping a journal, are so powerful. By helping young people notice patterns in their lives, self-reflection facilitates growth. The more you know yourself, and have a clear and honest record of your thoughts, the more you can grow.

4. **Debunking authority.** Adolescents are famous for their love of debunking authority. Pointing out mistakes made by parents or teachers is a particular delight. But they begin with huge blind spots here: they may accept the authority of a popular peer without question, or take the rules of a given group of friends as capital-T truth. This extends to their academics, too, for example with a tendency to believe the first Google search results they see.

For all of these reasons, joining them in their skepticism of authority can be a developmental antidote to conformity. You can help them question the quality of sources, or how someone knows something is true. This is a long game, but it can help a middle schooler avoid being stuck in the Belonging stage for too long, moving them toward the more complex thinking of what comes next: Achievement.

CHAPTER SUMMARY

* All of us, and particularly adolescents, have a deep need for belonging. Once we feel welcomed and accepted, we bring our full talents and capacities into action for our growth. Belonging defines the first developmental stage for most adolescents.

* Middle schools are unfortunately places where belonging and connectedness are often lost; we can change this by actively supporting adolescents in meeting the developmental tasks of this stage. Helping them find a peer group, giving them space to process what they're learning and wondering about with social

dynamics, and actively teaching social skills support them in successfully journeying through this stage.

* Some degree of conformity is normal developmentally, and adolescents may even seek to become nearly identical to close friends. This is healthy as long as they keep growing and don't stay in this conformist stage for multiple years.

* We can help them continue to grow by inviting them into groups that have different values, breaking the spell of conformity. We can share more of our own complex social lives, encourage self-reflection practices, and even encourage them to debunk authority, all of which help them become more sophisticated thinkers and navigators of the social world.

For Reflection

Recall a time in your adolescence when your sense of belonging was at stake—when you wanted badly to be part of a group or accepted in a certain way. How did this affect you, and how did you ultimately grow out of it?

_____

6

ACHIEVEMENT

We all feel it: the desire to be seen as excellent. Whether it's our highest hope or on the periphery of our lives, we all want the satisfaction of being skillful in an evident way, with others appreciating our abilities and accomplishments. This focus on achievement represents the next phase of the river, moving on from belonging as the key task. Two changes move adolescents forward into this next developmental stage.

The first change is, ideally, that they have completed the basic developmental work of the Belonging stage. They've begun to internalize a sense that they belong and feel confident that they can find and maintain friendships. This sense isn't ironclad—a move to a new school or a social or personal crisis could send them back to work on belonging again. But eventually, if things go well, they begin to feel more secure in this sense.

The second change is driven by the rapid brain development of early adolescence. With this growth comes the ability to make sense of more complexity. By mid- to late middle school, most students are not black-and-white thinkers anymore. They begin to be able to see shades of gray in arguments, even apparent paradoxes. They can detect more of the unspoken rules of groups, notice bias, and can see the games that both kids and adults play for social standing. They see that their "role" is actually multiple roles, that they show one side of themselves with a parent, another with their math teacher, and another with their best friend.

As they become more sophisticated thinkers, their motivations change. Earlier, in the Belonging stage, they may have felt safer with a small group whose rules they could understand concretely, even if those rules were stifling at times. But as they develop more complex thinking, they become more reflective and more skilled in seeing subtleties in how people interact. As other rules emerge out of the fog in front of them—*this teacher likes it when I use long words, this group will be impressed if I'm bold enough to sing on stage*—it's natural to want to test out these ideas and see if they can win respect in new ways.

As they grow, they don't discard past stages—they integrate them. An adolescent in the Achievement stage still wants to belong. They just are learning that they can belong in multiple groups, that they can enter and exit, without having their core sense of security shaken. They are moving on to the new challenges of achievement.

To return to our example of an adult moving to a new place to try a new profession: once you begin to feel confident that you are welcomed, that others believe you are in the right place, you find a sense of security and safety. It is common to next feel the drive to build competence, to show them what you can do. So it is for adolescents as well.

How can you tell if the adolescent in your life is entering or in the Achievement stage? Look for these markers:

1. **Social sensitivity and comparison.** In the Achievement stage, young people become even more aware of social norms, with more subtlety and nuance. They're prone to comparing themselves continually to peers, whether about grades, body development, popularity, athletic skill, or other qualities.

2. **Social mobility.** Adolescents in the Achievement stage realize they can be different with different groups—"I'm

one way around my music friends and another way around basketball friends." The farther they go into Achievement, the less this will trouble them, and it may feel like a mark of success that they can "make it" in very different spaces. They are now more able to move among groups.

3. **The drive to win.** In the Achievement stage, the core motivation is to be known as competent or as a "winner." This builds on their growing abilities to see what the rules are. The game they're exploring might be the popularity contest, or academics, or the best skateboarding moves, or access to the most elite high school. Each is akin to a drive for status. And while status may carry the negative connotation of being superficial, it is still an important stop on the developmental journey. If you don't believe you can be respected by others for your competence or success, it will be hard to move on to later stages of personal growth.

4. **Growing sense of agency.** Agency refers to the sense that you have control over the outcomes in your life and can exercise that control to make changes. In the Achievement stage, adolescents gain a greater sense of self-agency, together with growing abilities to plan and set goals. You may hear goals like "I want to be the fastest runner in my age class" or "This year I'm going to get a 4.0 GPA."

How Do We Support Them at This Stage?

As always, our task is not to rush them through a stage but to help them complete the developmental tasks of their current stage. For Achievement, this includes:

1. **Make sure there is at least one pursuit in which they feel valued, skillful, and on their way to mastery.** This can be in

any domain that has social credibility among at least some of the people in their life. It is extraordinary how much more confident and stable a person is once they feel secure in one area of mastery. It often enables middle schoolers to face areas of struggle with more resilience.

2. **Help them clarify the rules of different "games" in life.** At this stage, adolescents are keenly interested in learning the rules of all kinds of games that humans play. This might include the game of school, of friendships, of dating, of leadership, of activism, of athletic development, of theater, you name it. They have grown up in the middle of these many unspoken human rules, and now they are gradually seeing them, making sense of them, and deciding what they mean for their own path. "Instructing" them on the rules may create resistance, but being ready to talk through the rules with them, helping them check and clarify their observations, can be helpful and appealing.

3. **Help them experience healthy competition.** Adolescents at this stage are often highly competitive, driven by the desire to achieve and the tendency to constantly compare themselves to others. This creates one of the traps of this stage, which is to lose themselves in competition and begin valuing themselves entirely based on comparative scores of some kind. But some competition is healthy, and the drive is too strong to resist even if you wanted to. Instead, we do best by offering opportunities for healthy competition.

Resisting competition would be like refusing to feed someone who is hungry; encouraging rampant competition is like letting them loose at the candy store; offering healthy competition is like offering wholesome snacks.

So what is healthy competition? First, it means competition that everyone consents to joining. GPA is not a healthy form of competition since most students don't have a choice about receiving grades. Second, healthy competition offers objectivity: specific goals, clear rules for how you achieve them, and feedback to know where you stand relative to those goals. Third, care is taken that no one game is positioned to define your worth as a person. Rather, there are many games to choose among, and we can agree to play more than one, sometimes experiencing being the beginner and sometimes the winner.

At some point, even the Achievement stage, with its exciting competition and chances to play and win, will begin to lose appeal. Questions emerge: *Why am I playing this game anyway? Do grades even mean anything? What do I actually care about?* These questions may arise in adolescence or not until adulthood, when we begin to wonder why we've been hustling toward a goal we've been told is important. If an adolescent is lucky, though, they get to begin seeing the limits of the Achievement phase during their teen years, near the end of middle school or in high school. It can happen when the school they attend, or the people they spend time around, show that while achievement is important, it's not everything. To aim for more than achievement doesn't mean that achievement is pointless. Rather, achievement is a set of skills—like deducing rules, setting goals, and aligning resources—that you now have at your disposal, and which you can now direct toward the most worthy and personally authentic goals you can discover.

How Do We Challenge a Middle Schooler to Go Beyond This Stage?

When it seems they have been focused on achievement for a long time or when the toll of achievement, the stress or anxiety it can cause, is too evident, then it may be time to challenge an adolescent to go beyond this stage. Here are some suggestions:

1. **Help them see games as games.** Games are important, and much of life is about playing them well. But if we don't keep games in perspective, they threaten to consume us. We can help the young people in our lives play them well, and keep them in perspective, by speaking about parts of life as games, with strategies and tricks and ways to win.

   This can be particularly effective with games that create unhealthy stress, like the game of taking standardized tests. Here is a test that purports to measure overall intelligence but in reality, you can change your score dramatically by learning test-taking strategies and doing a few targeted forms of practice. So clearly it isn't only about intelligence. It's about how well you play this particular game. School is a game, college admissions is a game, and so on—each is playable, learnable, and not a measure of who you are.

2. **Question assumptions.** Adolescents in this stage may be more skillful in seeing social rules, but underneath that they may still accept without question that those rules are valid. For example, an academically driven student might be certain that grades are important, maybe the most import-ant thing in their lives. This can be fine, but if it's causing them harm, perhaps from high stress or the loss of other opportunities, some gentle questioning might be appropri-ate. Simply asking "Why?" for each level of response can go surprisingly deep. If grades are important to prepare for high school, which is important to prepare for col-lege, which gets you a job, which offers you money, which makes you happy . . . are we sure that's the only way to happiness? Unlike young people in the Belonging stage, at the Achievement stage adolescents are more scientific and

56

deductive in their thinking, so they tend to be more open to assumptions being challenged, as long as it's coming from the right source (alas, parents, this may not be you!).

3. **Show them differing examples of success.** You can begin here by holding achievement as a goal but taking apart the notion that there is one sure route. If an adolescent gets the idea that what really matters is acceptance into an elite college, say, then it may help to learn about or talk to someone who achieved extraordinary things and never went to college. You might even actively seek out and introduce them to interesting adults with nontraditional life paths. The aim is to develop a more complex appreciation for the many forms and paths of success. Few of us have linear, direct routes toward a goal in life.

   In the right moments, you may be able to invite them to question what success really is. Is it about money? Is it about happiness—and what does that word mean to you? Helping young people consider their own terms of success, and offering space and questions for those definitions to evolve, can help them avoid getting stuck in high-pressure, traditional achievement modalities.

   Your own modeling here matters greatly, as does that of other adults and peers. Do you live your life in such a way that achievement, with its external markers (degrees, money, popularity, etc.), appear to be the highest goal? Can you point to nontraditional stories of people you know— the rich friend who is not happy despite their wealth? The person who got fired but ended up then discovering a passion and a path unexpectedly?

4. **Build the confidence to wonder what's worth doing.** The concept of the growth mindset, made famous by Stanford professor Carol Dweck, refers to the belief that you can

grow with practice and change anything about yourself with effort. It is the opposite of a fixed mindset, in which you believe you either have a gift for something or you don't, and you can't change it. As Dr. Dweck and others have documented, a growth mindset enables us to achieve greater success by making us more resilient and determined learners, confident that we can expand our skills. You can encourage a growth mindset by modeling the importance of effort in gaining any skill. Being "not good" at a task really means "not good at it *yet*," as it's usually more a matter of practice than of innate talent.

This growth mindset is in some ways all about achievement, showing us that we can learn to win with enough practice. But when you take it deeply enough, it also sows the seeds of the next stage, beyond Achievement. Why? It's because when you realize you could achieve in almost any field, and learn almost any skill, the more relevant question becomes: *What is worth doing?* This is the turn of the river we've been looking for. Here comes the next stage: Authenticity.

CHAPTER SUMMARY

* Once they've completed their developmental tasks around Belonging, internalizing the security and confidence it offers, middle schoolers head toward the Achievement stage. In this phase they can use their growing social and cognitive abilities to figure out the rules to the games people play. They're aiming to show their abilities and gain status or respect from others.

* We can support adolescents at this stage by helping to make sure there is at least one pursuit, academic or otherwise, where they

feel skillful and on their way to mastery. The confidence from one clearly known strength can help them develop weaker areas.

* At some point, the less helpful sides of the Achievement stage become evident: the stress, the constant comparison with others, the rat race to win status. Students may begin to question the goals they've been told are important, like the validity of academic grades.

* We can invite them into the next stage by helping them see that there are many definitions of success, including some counterintuitive ones. We can speak about many competitive aspects of our world as games, with strategies to win, and develop their ability and belief that they can learn any game they want, leading to the question of which games are worth playing.

* Ultimately, the skills to achieve are extremely important, as are the skills to belong. But they are not the end of the road. The more interesting question becomes: To what end will I apply these skills?

For Reflection

When you were in middle school, what did you feel you were best at? Which skills were you proudest of? How did that evolve as you grew older?

7

AUTHENTICITY

I never really thought about my art making an impact on people. I never expected it to. But then I made an art piece about the Statue of Liberty and immigration for a class. Immigration just felt really relevant. We were hearing every day in the news about children in custody at the border. We wanted to make an art piece about it, but there were a lot of bumps in the road with the project. My partner and I made so many little sketches and designs, and drawing took a long time. It was hard. Finally, we created an art piece that showed the Statue of Liberty standing on a collage of cut-out images of politicians arguing about immigration.

Eventually it was time for the final presentation. Our class turned the school's multipurpose room into an art gallery and we set up our piece near the middle. I was nervous as people started to walk in. Students, parents, and teachers were looking around. Then I noticed people staring at our artwork and started to realize that people were really touched by what we had made. Someone started crying. It was like "Wow, a middle schooler did this?!"

At first I was confused because I didn't think it would really have an effect on people. I was kind of shocked, but also really proud. I know how art can really move me, and I want to be able to do that for others.

✳

This story was written by a seventh grader whose artwork on immigration said far more than words ever could. She was discovering and using her authentic voice. That's the heart of this next stage: if the Achievement stage teaches you to copy a great work of art, then the Authenticity stage enables you to create your own.

For some adolescents this stage opens as they discover their personal voice, as this student did. For others, it may come through questioning. *Why are we learning this?* or *What's the point of this?* are not necessarily rude remarks—they may be honest questions that signal a change is coming. An adolescent is seeing that trying to achieve more and more, winning grades or bringing home trophies, is no longer enough. They may wonder why achievement matters, and at some point, they will want to bring something more personal into the mix.

This is the third stage of our developmental river, termed Authenticity because of the drive to be yourself. In this stage, young people have integrated the experience and skills of Belonging and Achievement, with the resulting confidence that they can connect with others and get things done in the world. At some point, the question then becomes: *What is worth doing? Of all the games out there that I see people playing, which ones do I actually want to play? Which could I invent? What feels right to me regardless of how others see it?*

When you're secure in your abilities to belong and to achieve, a door opens. You may not walk through that door for years or even decades; there are many adults who learned in school that achievement (grades or looks or popularity, later perhaps money or degrees) is everything and don't stop to wonder why they're playing the game until they're hit with a midlife crisis or some other existential event. But if an adolescent is lucky, they'll notice while still young that achievement, while important, is not everything. When they begin to wonder about that, and particularly when they have the right context and support, they are walking through the door and out of the Achievement stage. They're about to access much more of their personal power and capability.

The Authenticity stage unlocks the full potential of a young person to be wise, loving, and capable. Think about it: if you are busy trying to be someone else (perhaps in order to belong to a group) or to win someone else's game (to show you have the best grades or skills), you are probably not tapping directly into your own genius. When you find your passions and accept them, cool or not, you are on the road to finding the greatest contributions you can make. You are discovering purpose and accessing the highest levels of personal motivation.

"Being yourself" may seem simple, especially if you think of younger children. But before puberty, most kids are far less attuned to the social consequences of their actions. They have not yet experienced that rude awakening into the social world, in which they realize they're constantly being judged, evaluated, and compared. To realize that and *then* choose to do something that is uniquely you and might seem weird to others—that is a powerful leap in development that can only happen after the transformative process of adolescence has begun.

You may also be wondering if this stage is really possible for middle schoolers or if it's more the province of adults who have the maturity to ponder such things. In my experience, this is another symptom of the low expectations our society holds for adolescents. If we give them meaningful challenges that speak to real-world issues, and if they have time and support to explore their inner emotional lives and their social worlds, then many adolescents will begin to advance beyond belonging and achievement as their core goals. They may begin to wonder *why* they're working so hard and *what* they're working toward. This is particularly true when they're in an environment that values and models authenticity, that tells them achievement is important but not the end of the road.

How can you tell an adolescent is entering the Authenticity stage? First, remember that earlier stages, before or at the very beginnings of puberty, can fool you by looking like the Authenticity stage. If an adolescent has not yet developed that intense focus on the social world and what others think, then they may seem effortlessly authentic because they haven't yet fully developed their social sensibility. It's only after gaining those social sensing abilities, triggered by the neurological changes of puberty, that they can begin working their way toward Authenticity. Here are some of the markers you may see:

1. *"I want to be me. You do you."* Statements like this indicate that they are starting to care less about whether others think they're cool and that being themselves matters more. It doesn't mean they're done with the tasks of Achievement, but they are beginning to see beyond it.

2. **Skepticism toward the game.** You may hear a version of "Grades may be important but there's more to life" or a questioning of one group's achievement goals, like not wanting to be part of a team if they only care about scoring. Or they may roll their eyes at something that used to worry them, like the popularity contest at school.

3. **Trusting quirky people.** At the Authenticity stage, many adolescents (or adults at this stage) have an easier time trusting people who are quirky and unusual. They may even feel suspicious of people who seem too "normal." Normal may seem like someone who is playing the achievement game without self-awareness. If the Belonging stage seeks sameness and Achievement prizes excellence, then Authenticity is more interested in the ability to honestly be yourself around others.

How Do We Support Them in Reaching This Stage?

As always, there is no rush to reach a stage on any particular time frame. The Authenticity stage requires a level of self-awareness that will arrive at a different time for each adolescent. Most can begin to explore it during the later stages of middle school, but it is equally normal if this door opens in high school. In any case, the ways we support it are similar, and we can begin setting the conditions well before an adolescent is ready for this phase. In fact, it's ideal if we do. Here is how we begin:

1. **Authentic adults.** Make sure there is at least one adult around them who seems authentically, weirdly, and happily themselves. If you are a parent and already model this, consider if there is a new source of adult influence that could be added to your child's life. Now is the time for branching out to new influences, and your role in curating those influences is powerful. This may mean finding an adult who could be an informal mentor or a group that operates with these values of acceptance and authenticity.

2. **Model that achievement is important but not the end of the road.** While we all want to inspire young people to work hard and set high goals, it is certainly possible to overdo this, drumming in goals like getting into selective colleges to such an extent that it may seem like that is what matters most or is how we'll ultimately judge their success. Instead, we can model that it's worth questioning what you are achieving for; that there are many different versions of success in adulthood; and that each person will ultimately be the judge of their own success. Our unconditional acceptance, regardless of status markers, means young people can spend less time worrying about or battling with our needs as adults and more time discovering their own talents, passions, and interests.

3. **Allow yourself to be more vulnerable.** Adolescents at this stage are beginning to see through you with more conscious awareness, making more accurate guesses at your real motivations. By showing more vulnerability—meaning that you choose to reveal more of your inner workings, more of your questioning and unfinished parts—you align your words with the subtle signals they pick up anyway, leading to more trust.

4. **Offer choice.** Even more than at previous stages, adolescents in this stage crave choice. They do not want to be hemmed in by one required way to do anything, whether it's a school project or their schedule on a weekend. It's important that they have greater freedom (always with responsibility) at this stage.

Keep in mind that we are far from finished with our development in middle school. Even the most evolved middle schooler is not likely to be fully in the Authenticity stage; they will have moments of struggling to belong or stressing about achievement. Or they may feel comfortable being their authentic selves by the time they're kings of the hill in eighth grade, only to return to something akin to a Belonging stage when they enter a new world in high school. All of this is normal.

We'll continue working on each stage, and perhaps others, throughout our lives. What's important is that our environment does not hold us back. For middle schoolers, that means that their adult and peer context should not stop them from growing through and beyond Belonging, through and beyond Achievement, and perhaps tapping into Authenticity. They'll gain a taste for it, perhaps sense how much personal satisfaction and capability lies in this stage, and thus find their way back to it more easily in future chapters of their adventure.

Remember that early adolescence, as a time of rapid brain growth, will have a more lasting influence on us than most other parts of our lives. It matters greatly what stages we are exposed to during these key years. If the context at home and in school models authenticity, then young people will not stop at achievement and will keep asking questions to discover their greatest contributions and passions. The point is not to be done with this quest—it's to become comfortable with the questions. With luck, they'll keep asking themselves what seems right to them, and what is worth doing, in each successive stage of life.

CHAPTER SUMMARY

* The third developmental stage for most adolescents is Authenticity, with its primary motivation to express who you are and your unique interests and skills regardless of what is seen as "cool" or given social status.

* In this stage, adolescents often become skeptical of grades or other traditional motivators or measurements. They may gravitate toward quirky adults or peers who seem to be authentically, and happily, themselves.

* While not all adolescents will reach this stage during middle school, we can serve them well by modeling that achievement is important but not the end of the road, and that there are many valid definitions of success.

* At this stage, adolescents connect well with adults who show vulnerability and honesty. They also prefer higher levels of choice, which enable them to keep exploring what is authentic to them.

* Ultimately, the Authenticity stage allows young people to tap into both more satisfaction and more real-world capability. In

following passions, they play to their strengths, develop unique depth in particular areas, and tap into their highest levels of personal motivation.

For Reflection

What is one part of your life right now where you feel most authentically yourself, playing to your strengths and passions? What is one part where you feel least authentic, like you are playing a game you would rather not play? Could you share these areas, and how they make you feel, with the adolescent in your life?

PART 2

BECOMING THE PARENTS MIDDLE SCHOOLERS NEED

In the first part of this book, we began to understand middle schoolers developmentally. Deeper than outer behaviors, comments, or daily ups and downs, a small number of core developmental drives motivate them: the quest for identity; the longing to connect with peers; and the need to feel valuable by contributing to real-world needs and problems.

With this frame we saw that as adolescents become more complex and social beings, they tend to go through certain stages. First they seek belonging, looking for safety and acceptance around others. Then they seek to achieve, to demonstrate valuable skills for others. And finally they seek authenticity, learning to be themselves among others, and through that they tap into their passions and full motivation.

When we understand middle schoolers in this developmental light, we can appreciate the battles they're facing and the needs they're seeking to meet. We can see them as perhaps we see ourselves—well-intentioned, struggling at times, but working hard for reasonable goals.

In this light we are less likely to take things personally. With any given behavior or comment, even a sarcastic or resistant one, we can trace it back to a developmental need. It's important that we do so, especially in difficult moments. Before we lose our temper or get caught up in judging or punishing, we can find the developmental source of the behavior. Then we know: they are trying to complete a developmental task. Perhaps we can help create the conditions for them to do this. Perhaps we can help them complete the task in more positive and productive ways. At the very least, we can avoid making their job harder.

Say for example that your child is telling you, "Give me some space," in more or less kind ways. A comment like that can sting. It can lead you to worry what they're doing with their time and which peers are influencing them. But before you go down those roads, you might ask yourself: What developmental need are they trying to meet by making that comment?

Perhaps they need more social time in their schedules. Perhaps they want to feel free to try on different identities and don't want you to see them until they are more confident. You can remind yourself that while the way they *express* their needs might need work, the needs themselves are understandable. Tell them that you'll be here when they want to connect later. This developmental understanding does not excuse rude behavior—but it does give you a basis to work with it more effectively.

In part 2, we'll apply this developmental lens to the adventure of parenting a middle schooler. How does it guide us to evolve our parenting? To support their physical health? To think about academics or beyond-school experiences? To navigate decisions around phones, social media, dating, and more? We can use this developmental perspective to reimagine and add new color to all of these areas.

We'll begin with perhaps the most important element: our shifting role in their lives.

Remember that they are on an intense journey. Whitewater rafting, dodging boulders, laughing wildly with their peers in the boat, surviving the thrilling and terrifying moments that come in rapid succession. When we have their full attention for a moment, what do they need from us? Not a lecture certainly, not a critical evaluation of their recent performance, and not withdrawal. What they need to find in us is an adult *companion*.

In earlier life they may have seen us as all-powerful beings (even when they tested limits), but things are changing now. They still need us. But if we pretend to be a boss with all the power, the result will often be intense conflict. Instead of a boss, they need wise and kind companions. This is the theme we'll explore next.

THE ART OF COMPANIONING

Here are two open secrets about parenting and teaching adolescents.

First: You are the curriculum. Every minute of the day, your words, actions, body language, and reactions transmit a huge volume of information to anyone around you. You're signaling how you see the world, manage stress, and solve problems; you're demonstrating mindsets about your growth, your body, how you face fears, what you value in others, and much more.

Enter middle schoolers, whose social radar is getting a huge upgrade as their brains develop. Practically every day, they can see a little deeper into the adults around them. They begin to see behind our masks. They're curious about what's really there, and what they'll be like as they grow older. They may not understand what they see behind those adult masks, but you can be sure they're picking it up and trying to make sense of it.

This means that, far more than the words we say or the formal lessons we teach, we offer *ourselves* as the real curriculum. It happens whether we want to or not. We are all highly imperfect *and* we are their models for adulthood. This is true whether that thought thrills or terrifies us, even whether we feel settled in our identity or not. Which brings us to number two.

Second: Adolescents are here to transform not only themselves but also you. Someone who is transforming is like a person on fire. If you spend enough time with them, you'll start to catch fire too. This might mean that you get triggered by certain things they do, full of fear or outrage. It might mean that parts of your own adolescence come roaring back out of your memory, replete with unfinished business, old hopes, or repressed experiences that still sting. It might mean a feeling of grief as you witness your own child moving away from you, growing into an adult, and your own empty nest in sight. It might mean that you yearn for their freedom or the opportunities they have ahead and, perhaps in connection with your own midlife wonderings, feel like shaking things up in your own life.

However it manifests for you, you can be sure that, unless you actively repress your inner self, raising or teaching an adolescent is going to stir things up within you. *This is their gift.* It's what you get in exchange for the emotionally intensive labor of helping them step into adult form.

What does this gift mean? Because you are the curriculum, a powerful model of what adulthood means, your own personal development becomes the most effective way to improve your parenting or teaching. In other words: they need to see you growing. You have the chance to walk side-by-side with them as fellow growing humans.

What a beautiful alignment this is, a reason to focus on your own growth and not sacrifice yourself for parenthood or teaching. By facing your own fears and developing new skills and friendships, you make yourself a more vibrant and relatable model for them, just as you are becoming a more vibrant human.

You don't have to give up all authority. In fact, this route opens a new form of authority, exercised by becoming an inspiring example and a bridge to the real world more than by issuing rules and punishments. Let's explore how we put this into practice, through the art of becoming a companion to those in transformation.

How to Accompany Someone

The three questions we explored in part 1—*Who am I? How do I connect? What will I contribute?*—are missions that adolescents are called to pursue. When you help an adolescent on their mission, you bring out their engaged, passionate, and motivated sides, which are much closer to their true nature than the stereotypical checked-out kid. The checked-out adolescent is often one who has concluded that adults don't know what matters and is trying to wait them out so that they can go back to the very important work of answering these questions.

If you want to help adolescents on their mission, you are volunteering as a companion on their adventure. At the heart of this is the way we see adolescents as heroes going on an epic journey of self-discovery. If we see them as brave adventurers, facing dangers and witnessing beauty, then we realize they don't need a boss hovering over them. They need a wise companion.

Consider this for yourself first. Imagine that you are embarking on a thrilling but perilous adventure. Say you are hiking along glaciers and over crevasses in the Arctic wilderness, setting up camp each night far from civilization. What kind of guide would you want?

You might want a guide who is dependable, trustworthy, and honest. Someone you can share a laugh with, or a cry. You might want someone who has awe for the terrain around you, able to gasp at the night sky.

You probably want a guide who knows the terrain. But how do they show that knowledge? Someone who is constantly explaining or warning you about every little danger is not ideal. They should be ready to accompany you when you explore somewhere new. They should proactively warn you about something only if there is real and present danger.

Your guide would not take your mistakes personally. They would have that healthy psychological distance (so hard for a parent or teacher to have, but we can aspire) that allows them to notice things without getting triggered or trying to fix you. They would wait for your questions before providing an answer they think you need.

Imagine this guide. These and other qualities that you would want are likely what an adolescent wants too. The journey is theirs. The identity forming is theirs. But their relationship to their guides— and whether they have a genuine guide—will matter greatly in how they discover themselves and how much they enjoy the process. This is your invitation to evolve. It's the role being offered to you to remain powerful and connected as a child begins the adventure of adolescence. You are now a companion.

Pitfalls on the Way

As we shift our mentality to that of a companion, we'll find both new opportunities and new traps. It's worth exploring a few of the more common pitfalls to keep them in mind for our natural moments of struggle.

* **Pretending to be a peer.** Sometimes we might overcorrect, trying to go all the way from an authoritarian parent, or from a traditional teacher, to pretending to be a peer. This comes from a good place, from a desire to connect and remain close. But you are not a peer, and they know it. They need to figure out social dynamics with actual peers while redefining their relationships with adults. Creating an artificial situation in which an adult tries to become a peer-like buddy only leads to confusion. It may even cause harm by slowing down their social learning.

* **Becoming a secret boss.** We may be tempted to try to control things from behind the scenes. Here, too, we are in for trouble. The mistake is overconfidence that you know the best route for them through the wilderness. You may be

drawing on your adolescence here, or that of other young people you are reminded of, and thus think you know what your child needs. But it is their journey, and their struggles and hopes may be different from what you imagine. It is far better to be present, available, and ready to support rather than attempting to design each step of their journey for them.

✳ **Disappearing.** A final pitfall worth mentioning is that of withdrawing. This can be a well-intended correction that goes too far, in hopes of giving them space; or it can be a resentful disappearance, stung by the way they push back gracelessly or argue endlessly. Either way it's a trap. For as peer-motivated as they are, adolescents still deeply need adults. They just need those adults in different ways. They need examples of what healthy adulthood is. They need a shoulder to cry on at times. Most will need your help to create the right conditions for their personal discovery and growth.

So, if you can't be a peer, can't be the boss even if in secret, and can't just disappear and let them figure it out, what are you to do? Here are some companioning skills to try.

1. **Learn to be an active witness.** This is one of the most essential companioning skills. It begins by understanding something that may seem paradoxical: middle schoolers often want you there, but they also want you to be in the background. Too much adult voice or control can aggravate them, whether because they feel babied, watched, or simply stifled in getting to explore as they wish. So if you are to be present with them, you have to accept a mostly background role. This is the role of the active witness: someone who demonstrates that they are present by paying attention, but

who does not react, judge, or intervene except in the most serious circumstances.

2. **Locate your baggage.** We all carry psychological baggage, the accumulation of old wounds, past crises that still make us fearful about particular risks, plus our preferences and biases from the particular route we've walked so far in life. If we're not aware of this baggage, it's likely to show up at the least ideal times. It may create conflict with the adolescent we're trying to accompany or flood us with unexpected emotion when we want to be present for them. This is part of the invitation to pursue our own personal growth to better parent or teach adolescents. If you haven't yet had the opportunity to work with a therapist and have the privilege to do so, this is the time to get one. If a therapist is not affordable or available, consider if there are circles of friends with whom you can be extremely honest, who can function as a support group for each other's growth as parents or teachers.

3. **Accept the invitations coming.** You're going to receive many invitations for your own growth. How will you know when they arrive? Simple: look for emotion. After all, intriguing neuroscience research suggests that emotions result from times when our brain made an incorrect prediction. When something is exactly as we expect, we often don't feel much emotion. When it is better or worse, we may feel happiness, anxiety, or more. In other words: emotions indicate the opportunity to learn. Look for the times when your emotions come out strongly around the middle schooler(s) in your life. Maybe you suddenly have a strong wish for them, are infuriated by something they say, or feel anxious that they aren't proceeding fast enough. Each of these is an invitation for your personal growth. What is it

about you, your past, or your hopes for them that is causing such a strong reaction?

As you explore these questions, you have the chance both to evolve personally and to align yourself with your child or student. You become a fellow learner, able to be humbled and thrilled and surprised by the daily twists in your path.

4. **Find a more generous relationship with time.** Many adults living in modern society have developed an anxious attitude toward time, and it's often clear in how we parent. Intentionally or not, we end up trying to control our kids with time. We push them to go faster, finish up quickly, or end one activity prematurely to begin another. It can lead to adolescents becoming passive, because their schedules or the reminders from adults are so constant that there is hardly a chance for them to lose themselves in their own interests. It can lead to missing valuable opportunities, like a middle schooler making dinner or fixing something they broke, because we don't have time for them to tinker, make mistakes, and learn through practice.

To borrow from our earlier example, you probably would not want a wilderness guide who was constantly rushing you to the next sight. To be wise companions, we need to find greater ease with time. This may mean working to notice the time anxiety we feel within, so that we don't impose it unintentionally on our children. There will still be moments worthy of adding urgency, but choose those moments carefully and appreciate the value of being immersed in an experience without the pressures of time.

5. **Don't do this alone.** In times of great change, isolation can be scary. It's hard to know what is OK and what to be concerned about; it's hard to steady yourself through the

ups and downs if there is no one to lean on or reflect with. Sadly, far too many parents have no meaningful support group of fellow parents, especially during the years when their children become adolescents.

We can change this. In fact, this is one of the very first steps to transform our experience of raising middle schoolers. It is essential to find fellow parents who are willing to have more than casual conversations about their kids, who can honestly share, discuss without judgment, and laugh and cry together through the journey. It may be possible to join or create a middle school parents group to exchange tips, ask for advice, and feel like part of a team on a shared journey.

CHAPTER SUMMARY

* Let's not pretend that the formal curriculum we teach young people is what they're primarily absorbing. They're absorbing *us*, the adults accompanying them, far more. When we accept this, we realize our own growth and development is key, helping us be the most vibrant models of adulthood possible and placing us alongside adolescents as fellow learners.

* We may be used to thinking of ourselves as the boss or manager, but with adolescents, a better metaphor is that of companion or guide. Think of who you would want alongside you on a difficult wilderness trek—these qualities may define the new role we can take on for the adolescents in our lives.

* As we hear the call to transform, a few false paths may appear. We need to avoid three traps here: pretending to be a peer, trying to secretly be the boss, or simply withdrawing.

* Learning to be a companion is an art. It involves being able to witness someone without trying to fix them. It challenges us to

work on our own psychological baggage. Finally, it should push us to find or create a supportive group of fellow parents, as we can't reach our own potential in isolation.

For Reflection

Think back to your middle school years, and imagine that the ideal guide or mentor appeared one day and was able to help you in exactly the way you most needed. What would the qualities have been of this person?

9

BODY UP

Our brains, wonders of the universe that they are, sometimes take up a little too much of our focus when we think about education. Why else would we design schools in which we're largely seated, motionless, during learning time, as if the body is a distraction or a device that we can turn off? Why else would schools put such a low priority on the quality of the food they serve or the quality of movement time, regularly cutting the budget and minutes allocated to PE? We seem to think we can do business brain-to-brain, when really we connect and grow as embodied humans.

Enter middle schoolers. If we want to make sense of them, and if we want to be the most effective and wise companions, we have to see them as physical beings. What are their natural rhythms, their needs for sleep, nutrition, and movement? How many of these needs are they meeting now?

If we follow this path, we'll come to appreciate that more of their behavior is driven by physical sensations and needs than we might think. As psychologist Mona Delahooke describes in her book *Beyond Behaviors,* we systematically overestimate how much top-down, intentional choice is in the behaviors we see in young people, and we underestimate how much behavior is "body-up," driven by signals from our bodies. These may be signals around the need to move or sleep, feelings of stress or perceived threat, or our unique ways of processing sensory information coming in. Understanding these signals is key to interpreting behavior correctly. Otherwise, we are likely to be frustrated by assuming willful choices where there may be none, or by giving out critiques or punishments that actually make things worse.

In this chapter, we'll consider four questions about middle schoolers' physical habits. Before we go any further, it's important to say that this is not a book about physical health, and I am not a doctor. I'm writing with my educator hat firmly on, pointing out the times when I've seen middle schoolers struggle or thrive based on physical habits. Please consult a doctor before making any major changes around health practices.

Let's begin with the area where I've seen the greatest challenge for middle schoolers, and thus perhaps where we'll find the greatest room for improvement.

How Are They Sleeping?

When our kids were tiny, their sleep was a subject of intense interest. Maybe because their sleep determined our sleep as parents—or because it so clearly set them up for a good or bad day ahead. And in early childhood, that time of incredibly rapid physical and brain growth, their needs for sleep were particularly high. But remember that other highest time of physical and brain change in life? That would be early adolescence, and it's when their sleep needs again leap up. Here, too, it's worthy of our attention as parents.

Adolescents need more sleep than elementary schoolers or adults. Their bodies and brains are developing at a phenomenal clip. According to current research, most adolescents need nine to ten hours of sleep per night. Those who consistently get less sleep have higher rates of anxiety and depression, as well as more emotional volatility, behavior challenges, and difficulty learning.

But here, unlike early childhood, we have more to contend with than gassy babies or middle-of-the-night feeds. Something is going very wrong with adolescent sleep habits. Chronic sleep deprivation has become the norm for middle and high schoolers. Let's explore the reasons why.

First, among the brain changes of puberty is one that leads adolescents to have a shifting body clock, or circadian rhythm, causing them to naturally fall asleep later and want to sleep in later. This shift toward more night-owl behavior begins at the onset of puberty and continues moving their clocks later and later until the effect peaks somewhere in their late teens to age twenty.

Second, we know that due to other brain changes orienting them toward peers, most middle schoolers have an essentially limitless social appetite. If they have a phone or other device that lets them message friends or be on social media, it will be very hard for them to decide when they've had enough social time and turn it off at night.

Third, we adults are the culprits in often giving excessive homework or overstuffing their schedules with activities. While well-meaning, these choices can lead middle schoolers to be doing homework until well into the night; if they have an understandable desire to relax or connect before bed, they may have no other time to do that but late at night.

These three forces make it easy to stay up later and later, but then adolescents meet an immovable object: school start times. Since sleeping in is impossible during the weekdays (and sleeping in only on the weekends does not, according to research, make up for weekday sleep deprivation), adolescents will generally wake up before their bodies are really ready. The American Pediatric Association recommends that middle and high schools start at 8:30 A.M.

at the earliest, but most start earlier, and parents often need to get to work earlier.

The result is that adolescents show up at school with too little sleep, too early in the day for their circadian rhythms. A staggering 66 percent of adolescents in the United States are chronically sleep-deprived. One has to wonder, looking at the high rates of emotional volatility and mood disorders in teens, how much of this stems from sleep deprivation?

Depressing research aside, we do have some levers to pull to change this situation:

1. **Advocate for later school start times.** This is not a quick or simple process, but that shouldn't stop us from setting it as a long-term goal. It's what is best for adolescents. Take it from the American Pediatric Association: "Insufficient sleep represents one of the most common, important, and potentially remediable health risks in children, particularly in the adolescent population, for whom chronic sleep loss has increasingly become the norm." There is a growing movement to shift middle and high school start times later, and with luck and effort this will continue.

2. **Remember that they may not mean to be night owls.** Many a parent has been frustrated at their middle schooler for staying up too late, perhaps assuming that it's a lack of care about school or general surliness that is prompting their night-owl behavior. Perhaps those elements are at play, but a more likely explanation is that their bodies are changing and that makes it harder for them to fall asleep earlier, plus they may be enjoying a chance to socialize or play. While good sleep hygiene (see below) and other practices can help, you can't entirely stop the natural developmental process that will shift their body clocks to be more night-oriented. They are not choosing to be like this—it's a neurological

change they're grappling with. If we can avoid taking it personally, we can approach this like any other physical change they're going through.

3. **Learn sleep hygiene practices.** Because most schools still start too early, adolescents will sleep as late as possible until they have to wake up for school. Any improvements in their sleep are thus about getting to sleep earlier. Research has shown it is possible to make significant changes here, using what's called sleep hygiene. Here are some research-backed tips for parents:

* Set a bedtime of 10 P.M. or earlier, which is correlated with better mental health outcomes for adolescents.

* If they consume caffeine from coffee, tea, soda, or energy drinks, try to reduce the overall amount.

* Have consistent mealtimes.

* Stop any screen time thirty to sixty minutes before bed.

* Use light exposure: exposure to bright, ideally natural light starts our body clock for the day. The earlier in the morning we have light exposure, the earlier that night we'll begin to feel sleepy.

4. **Help adolescents draw their own conclusions.** As is true for any of us, if we come to a conclusion from our own experience and thinking, we'll resist it less and remember it longer than if we were simply told the answer. Middle schoolers are capable of being given scientific research on sleep, making sense of it with assistance, and testing it out in their own lives. In fact, some of the most powerful ways I've seen to teach the scientific method have involved exactly this: an invitation for students to create experiments on themselves, working with variables in their control (like when they turn

out the lights at night), and studying outcome variables like how they feel the next morning. I've even seen middle schoolers conduct this research and then package it into a parent education evening. Imagine how much more open-minded they feel when *they* are the ones presenting the sleep recommendations.

What Are Their Senses Telling Them?

We may have similar sensory equipment like our eyes and ears, but we don't experience our senses in the same way. We each have a unique set of sensitivities. I may be easily distracted by loud noises but oblivious to the textures of foods. You may be tuned to the visual environment and easily bothered by clutter. None of these are clinical disorders, but they are key differences in how we see the world, as distinct in combination as our personality.

It turns out that these sensitivities matter greatly in parenting and in designing learning environments. Take a child who tends to be attuned to sound and is easily bothered by unexpected or chaotic noises: if their classroom is loud and noisy, they may feel a sense of threat on a visceral level. We shouldn't be surprised, then, if they are distracted, show difficulty focusing on the topic at hand, or have trouble managing their emotions. If we respond by punishing them, we are adding more problems to their plate, when the root challenge may be sensory. This is what Dr. Delahooke meant by saying that we assume too many behaviors are top-down when really more are body-up.

What does this mean? If we want to guide the middle schooler in our lives, we need to understand their sensitivities, and then help them manage these sensitivities. For example, you wouldn't expect a very shy child to love going to a big party, though if it was important and they had some support, they could manage it. Similarly, with sensory differences, if you know you're heading into an environment that will make it harder to control your emotions or behavior, you can prepare strategies and fare much better as a result.

Since a key part of our job as wise companions is to set the conditions for a young person's growth, we can put this awareness of their sensitivities to use. For that acoustically sensitive child, we may want to help them create a calm, quiet study spot at home. For a child who is easily frustrated by visual noise or clutter, we could help them create excellent organizational systems so that their bag, binders, or planners are well set up. We can help young people become aware of situations that may be triggering—not to avoid them but to prepare strategies so that they can still be calm and content in those moments.

There's one last piece—and this may be the best part. Your sensitivities are not just triggers you have to manage. There's a compelling case to be made that they are the doorway to your gifts. In the wonderful book *Radical Wholeness*, author Philip Shepherd argues that our sensitivities are a form of intelligence. He describes sensitivities as your stockpiles of raw intelligence, waiting for you to refine them into a more usable form. Each sensitivity, refined through practice and effort, can lead you to discover an unusual ability or insight. That sensitivity to the visual world, clutter and all, may represent the raw materials for advanced skills in the arts or design, as just one of many examples. For a middle schooler questing to discover who they are and how they can make a contribution, these insights may be priceless.

How Are They Eating?

It goes without saying that the food we eat affects us both in the moment—perhaps causing us to be sleepy after a large, heavy meal or to race with energy after eating a candy bar—and in the long run, as our food choices accumulate to form the very bodies we live in.

In her groundbreaking book on the neuroscience of emotions, *How Emotions Are Made*, neuroscientist Lisa Feldman Barrett makes a powerful point: if we want to get better at managing our emotions, we have to look at our physical health first. Eating nutrient-dense foods enables our brains to smoothly manage functions like metabolism, heart rate, and blood pressure. Feldman Barrett's research shows us that this ability to more consistently manage our energy needs leads to more positive emotional states. Indeed, she suggests that how well our brain predicts our body's needs may be the origin of much of our underlying emotional state.

Middle school is the time of greatest emotional volatility in our lives, so if our eating choices can make emotions more manageable, they deserve our full attention. Indeed, in studies of adolescents, foods that cause less variation in our blood sugar levels (known as low-glycemic-index foods) predict better alertness, happiness, and confidence and even lead to improved scores on tests of memory. Food that has higher nutrient value, is less processed, and has a lower glycemic index will help adolescents be the best version of themselves.

Knowing this, how can we help?

1. **Turn eating into a research project.** Sermons on healthy eating are not likely to win over most middle schoolers. But we have another option, one that is more respectful to their growing skills as well as more effective: engage them in research. Inviting middle schoolers to learn about food research, or to conduct self-experiments, can help them draw their own personal correlations between diet and mood, focus, or other outcomes.

2. **Make good snacks available.** It doesn't take a research study to know that middle schoolers get hungry—a lot. All of that rapid growth and development takes energy. One simple tactic, whether for educators or parents, is to make healthy, low-glycemic-index snacks the only options available. You may not be able to win out in a head-to-head competition with Doritos, but if your healthy snack is the

only game in town, chances are many middle schoolers would rather satisfy their hunger than wait.

3. **Make time to eat.** While this may sound obvious, some kids' schedules, both at school and after school, are so full that they don't have enough time to eat. Too many schools squeeze lunch into a twenty-minute period, which may also represent the only open socializing time a student has in a day. If they are not getting their social needs met elsewhere, or are now immersed in the intense social environment of a cafeteria, it is likely they will not focus on their food. As *Education Week* wrote, "By the time students walk to the cafeteria, maybe run to the bathroom, and wait in line for their food, they often don't have enough time to eat all of their meal—especially the healthy, more fibrous parts— which can have long-lasting effects on their academic per- formance and behavior."

   Research points to lengthening school lunchtime as the solution to this. At home, research also indicates that having family meals together leads to better eating (in terms of the food's nutritional value) among adolescents. As we'll explore in chapter 18, the spirit of *generosity with time* is a key that unlocks many benefits.

4. **Stay alert to eating disorders.** Any time you invite middle schoolers to explore questions of food and diet, keep a watchful eye for signs of eating disorders. These are among the most common and dangerous mental health condi- tions that can afflict adolescents. Open conversation about our relationship to food and to our bodies is a powerful tool to prevent eating disorders, as well as a way to notice signs they may be emerging. If your child wants to use food choices to lose weight, make sure they have a doctor's approval and guidance.

How Are They Moving?

As with each other section in this chapter, the research on exercise and adolescents easily merits a book of its own. As you might guess, the results are powerfully in favor of more exercise. Physical activity in adolescents predicts better sleep quality, better mental health, and even improvements in their cognitive abilities. It's notable that exercise seems to have a particularly positive effect on the cognitive abilities known as executive function, which most middle schoolers struggle with. This includes their abilities to organize, plan, set goals, and stay focused. The effect on executive function seems to be particularly strong when the exercise is cognitively engaging, for example, a game that involves strategy, collaboration, and movement at the same time.

Many parents and teachers are already convinced of the merits of exercise but struggle with a more practical question: How do we encourage middle schoolers to exercise more? Here are some ways to begin:

1. **Make it social.** Trying to force exercise or moralize about it will have limited results at best. Far better is to tap into middle schoolers' powerful social drive. The chance to be part of a team or to belong to a group that shares an interest, such as yoga, could be the most compelling reason to begin exercising. Middle schoolers are more likely to show up regularly because of the bonds formed in these experiences, which fortunately are ideal situations for making friends.

2. **Offer choice.** Middle schoolers are likely to bristle at a demand to exercise in a particular way. Instead, offer as much choice as possible. For example, you might set the parameters with a family rule that each September, everyone tries a new sport—but then offer maximum flexibility to choose what sport they'd like to try. Keeping in mind

their social drive, it may help to note which friends are doing which sports or activities, as this could be the most relevant piece of information for their choice.

3. **Take developmental stage into account.** For a middle schooler looking for belonging, exercise doesn't matter a hundredth as much as feeling accepted. So bring the two together. The goal may be to find your people by testing out different sports and activities. For someone at the Achievement stage, sports or exercise often suit them perfectly. They may enjoy competitive sports, particularly once they find one where they feel the potential to excel. Innovative PE programs may offer tools like wearable body sensors, in which students can track physical metrics like heart rate during an activity and work to improve their numbers over time. For students at the Authenticity stage, exercise may be more about fun and self-expression, and they may enjoy discovering unusual games or activities.

4. **Advocate for high-quality, regular PE.** Too many schools have cut back on PE to increase "seat time" in academic classes—a telling phrase. Because middle schoolers often prefer to use recess times for socializing, it's essential that they have regular PE to ensure there is movement and health education happening. Ideally, PE would take place daily and would offer a wide range of activities so that each student can find some that they enjoy.

Bringing It All Together

We have to see middle schoolers as physical beings. When we include questions of physical wellness, habits, and sensitivities, we become far wiser companions to them.

Without being carried away by every latest research finding, we can aim to live healthfully for ourselves first—knowing that we are the curriculum—and we can gently raise our children's or students' awareness of their own physical health. By introducing them to the research and inviting them to conduct thoughtful experiments, we convey that they are in charge of their bodies and their health, and that much about their focus, mood, and energy level is changeable based on choices and effort.

Each step we make—whether a slightly more nutrient-rich diet or a shift to later school start times—will contribute to an overall improvement in health. In a Canadian study looking at lifestyle recommendations for early adolescents, including sleep, diet, and exercise, researchers found that for each recommendation being followed, there was a 15 percent decrease in the number of physician visits for mental health. In other words, each step matters. Take one step at a time.

———————— CHAPTER SUMMARY ————————

* To understand a middle schooler, we need to understand their physical self. What are their bodily habits and needs? Their physical, reflexive responses are responsible for more of their behavior than we might think—in other words, their actions are often more body-up than top-down.

* Sleep is a natural beginning point. Shifting circadian rhythms, the lure of technology, and too-early school start times combine to make sleep deprivation all too common among adolescents. We can improve this with better sleep hygiene, limits on nighttime technology use, and by advocating for middle schools to start at 8:30 A.M. or later.

* We each have a personal set of sensory differences as complex and unique as our fingerprints. Understanding these, and helping a young person discover them, unlocks many ways to improve focus, reduce stress, and tap into new forms of intelligence.

* What we eat has a large impact on not only our long-term health but also our moment-to-moment emotional well-being. We can help make sure middle schoolers have enough time to eat, good snacks available during the day, and the chance to conduct their own self-experiments around how food affects their well-being.

* Exercise affects how adolescents think, how well they focus in school, how they sleep, and at heart how psychologically well they feel. We can help through our own modeling around exercise, advocating for exercise time during the school day, and by arranging for students to be invited by peers to participate in sports or movement activities.

For Reflection

Looking back on your own middle school years, what were your physical habits around sleep, diet, and exercise? If you could have made one change, how could it have helped you?

Among your physical senses, what are you especially sensitive to? Does this sensitivity lead to particular struggles and/or to certain gifts or insights? What sensitivities do you see in your child?

INNER WORK

For years now I've had a quote on my desk, surviving where other quotes have come and gone. It's attributed to Meister Eckhart, and it goes like this:

> *If the inner work is small, the outer work cannot be great.*
> *If the inner work is great, the outer work cannot be small.*

I've turned to this again and again for reassurance. It reminds me to tend to myself. It helps me avoid the cult of productivity. The inner work—the attempts to understand and manage the complex world of thoughts and emotions within—is primary. It activates the skills we need to do anything good in the world. To focus our attention. To calm ourselves. To have insight into our feelings. To notice our habits.

As important as inner work is for adults, it may be even more essential for adolescents. After all, they're changing far faster than we are. Their bodies, intellects, emotions, and social world change radically, sometimes by the day. They regularly gain new abilities of social perception but don't yet have the experience to temper them. If they learn how to manage their inner world, they can gain insight into these new feelings, notice their evolving habits, focus their attention, and calm themselves. Without attending to their inner world, they are in for a much rougher ride.

In case anyone feels these skills are too soft or a distraction from academics, consider these examples.

What if a bad test score floods you with such intense and unmanageable emotions that you run out of the classroom to hide and cry in the bathroom? I know this one—this was me in seventh grade. What if a friend's thoughtless comment sends you into a spiral of despair, and you try to ignore the feelings but are so preoccupied by them that you tune out the rest of your classes that day? I could cite a hundred more examples. Without the ability to calm and focus themselves, adolescents will be continually distracted from school and even from their own personal values.

If you still need convincing, a mountain of research supports this point: how well young people manage their social and emotional worlds has an immense impact on their success in school, among friends, and eventually in adult life.

In study after study, results show that when young people are offered social-emotional learning (SEL) tools to manage emotions, resolve conflicts, generate focus on goals, and more, they become happier and less anxious. Their test scores increase. They report better social lives. They show greater connectedness to school. The list goes on. Other research shows that these benefits persist into adulthood, with lower rates of mental health disorders and strong correlations with career success.

The education world has begun to catch on. Since the 1990s, SEL has gone from a largely unknown topic to one of the most influential new focus areas in schools. Let's examine the SEL research and see how it might inform our parenting.

Traits or Skills?

There is something deeply optimistic about the field of social-emotional learning, and it comes from one particular mental leap. That leap is from *traits* to *skills*. Simply put, it used to be thought that many social and emotional skills were innate, something you were born with, perhaps part of your personality. This was the trait view—you have it or you don't. It said that some people are going to be better at connecting with others, and some are just bound to struggle managing their own emotions.

The more optimistic view, and thankfully the one supported by research, is that most social and emotional abilities are teachable *skills*. While there are real differences in temperament, like introversion or extroversion, these do not stop you from developing high levels of social and emotional skill with the right teaching and support.

In other words, just about everyone can significantly increase their social-emotional skills with practice and gain the many benefits that result. What's more, the window of opportunity for this learning is particularly open during middle school. With rapid brain changes creating new social insight and new emotional complexity, middle school is going to be a formative time for our social perspectives and emotional patterns no matter what. With good SEL teaching, it can be a formative time in the most positive sense.

What Can They Learn?

You could fill many shelves with books on social-emotional learning and curricula. To avoid an avalanche of information, think of these skills as being in four categories:

* **Self-awareness** covers abilities like understanding your personality and your emotional world, as well as becoming self-reflective, savvy about mental health, and aware of the supports around you.

* **Self-management** builds on your awareness and includes skills to manage your emotions, set and work toward goals, make thoughtful decisions, handle failure, and focus your attention.

FINDING THE MAGIC IN MIDDLE SCHOOL

* **Social awareness** skills enable you to be aware of others' emotions, read situations and participate accordingly, notice bias in your thinking, and be able to hold multiple points of view.

* **Social management** includes the skills to make and maintain friendships, listen deeply, function well in teams, resolve conflicts, generate empathy, and use tools like gratitude and forgiveness to strengthen relationships and improve mental health.

In an ideal middle school journey, students would be introduced to these skills when they are relevant, meaning when real-world situations, like academic stress or friendship conflict, make such tools immediately useful. In this ideal world, SEL skills would be presented as equally important to academic skills, and they would be modeled by the adults around them. It's not necessary that every middle schooler master every SEL skill—but the more of them they have the chance to put into practice, the better they'll fare in school, in social life, and at home.

How Do We Teach These Skills?

1. **Modeled behavior.** The vast majority of social-emotional skill building is informal and unconscious. It's a constant background process of watching others and absorbing their behaviors, reactions, emotional patterns, unspoken beliefs and biases, social strategies, and more. So it follows that for adults looking to teach these skills, most of the work is in living them in our own lives.

   How can we model and reveal the social-emotional tools we use to get by? Much of the work involves taking internal, or behind-closed-doors, processes and gradually revealing them. Can you talk about your conflicts and how you resolve them, instead of attending to them privately? Can you acknowledge your emotional swings and share your tools for managing them? Can you model acceptance, curiosity, and empathy in response to someone else's ups and downs?

2. **Facilitated peer groups.** One of the most powerful forms of SEL, though still a relatively rare one, is the experience of being in a facilitated peer group. This is ideally a small (six to twelve students) and consistent group of young people, facilitated by a trained adult, in which participants have a safe space to share what's going on in their lives, learn and test out social-emotional tools, and find ways to support each other and make sense of adolescence together.

   Some schools work toward this goal through advisory programs, and we'll explore how to do this in chapter 16. Unfortunately, advisory is usually *not* like this in most schools and often defaults to being a time for administrative announcements and homework. Parents can still find opportunities, sometimes through supplemental or after-school programs (see chapter 14). And teachers can still bring these skills into their homeroom or advisory periods with the right training and support.

3. **Freedom of identity.** Middle schoolers are natural experimenters, often testing out different identities. The more we enable them to experiment, with less cost to their experiments, the more likely they are to discover which identities feel most authentic (and to build a habit of continually asking and answering that question anew). The more they can do this, the more their natural motivation, skillfulness, and charm will flow freely, rather than being diverted by attempts to be someone they aren't. Our task is to avoid making fun of or repressing their identity experiments, unless they are actively harming others. Remember that

when they are experimenting with identities, they are doing their developmental work.

We may be able to help them by suggesting groups, activities, or communities to try joining (or, better yet, arranging for them to be invited by a peer). And without casting a blind eye on internet usage, we can accept that for all the dangers of wandering through online communities, for many middle schoolers these are places where they can learn about and try on different identities. We'll explore this more in the next chapter.

4. **Reflection practices.** At the heart of many social-emotional tools is the ability to self-reflect. A reflection practice such as journaling provides solace, space to wonder and process, and the chance to become more metacognitive, or aware of our own thoughts. In a family or classroom, a reflection practice also builds our tools of description. Intriguing research shows that the more clear and specific our language around emotions, the better we are at managing those emotions, perhaps because the language pushes us to understand them more deeply and enables better communication.

5. **Conflict-resolution tools.** Conflict contains the ingredients for some of the most memorable learning as adolescents: it is socially focused and emotionally charged. How middle schoolers experience conflict will shape their identity. So we should see conflict as a golden opportunity to teach social and emotional skills. There are many tools here, but some of the best come from Restorative Justice and Nonviolent Communication practices. The right conflict-resolution tool will help adolescents become aware of subtleties like the difference between facts, emotions, and assumptions, all of which might be at play in the same moment of conflict. In addition to the learning, the confidence generated from

being able to repair friendships or team collaborations is of great value.

─────────── CHAPTER SUMMARY ───────────

* The research is clear: social-emotional intelligence is central to our success in school and in our adult lives. Thankfully, it's not something you're either born with or not; social-emotional intelligence is a set of skills that can be taught and practiced.

* The rapid brain development and identity evolution in middle school make it an optimal developmental window to learn these skills. Middle schoolers can become sophisticated navigators of their social and emotional worlds. We can hold high expectations in this regard, provided that we give them time and support to learn social-emotional skills and make mistakes along the way.

* We can support middle schoolers' social-emotional development first with the behaviors we model for them, then by finding the right experiences, like a facilitated peer group, where they can speak honestly about their social and emotional dilemmas. There's nothing like an SEL tool offered when you need it most. Beyond this, we can support their freedom of identity by accepting their natural identity experiments, modeling self-reflection practices, and leaping at the opportunity to address conflicts, which offer lasting social-emotional lessons.

For Reflection

When you were in middle school, what were some of the challenges that came up around emotions or your relationships (whether with peers, teachers, family members, etc.)? What skills do you wish you had?

11

FRIENDS

Eric and Joaquin, two sixth-grade boys, were frenemies. They enjoyed joking around but also got on each other's nerves. Eric wanted a friend, but somehow the ways he tried to connect often annoyed Joaquin. At break times they played dodgeball, and it seemed like they were always on the border between fun and frustration. One day it finally broke open. Eric threw a dodgeball that hit Joaquin square in the face. Joaquin roared with rage and ran after Eric, looking ready to brawl. Luckily, other students intervened before any punches were thrown. But it seemed like a fight was inevitable.

After talking the boys down, we deployed our whole range of conflict-resolution tools. Nothing seemed to work. We moved all the way to our highest-level intervention: the entire sixth grade, consisting of twenty-four students, had a meeting for conflict resolution. They heard the boys describe their grievances and set a goal for more peace, and the whole grade then agreed to take concrete steps to help them. Finally, the conflict seemed to abate, and we adults were relieved.

Curiously, for some time, neither of them found other friends. It dawned on us that, for all the friction their interactions had created, Eric and Joaquin were actually natural friends. Both were quirky, emotional, earnest kids with good senses of humor.

It took until the end of the year, but it finally happened. One day someone noticed that, during the entirety of a recess time, Eric and Joaquin were walking around the perimeter of the gym together, lost in conversation. They looked for all the world like two old men strolling a park, chatting about life. To our delight, this became their norm—day after day the next school year, they could be found walking the perimeter of the gym.

I think of this as a classic tale of middle school friendship. Friction is often involved. The boundaries are blurry between playful and aggravating ways to connect. There is a volatility to middle school friendships that can cause no end of frustration both for young people and the adults caring for them. But there are a few mindsets that can help us shift our stance.

First, we know from brain science that this is inherently a socially focused time in life. Middle schoolers' very identity is being redefined based on their social lives. So the intensity is high, but for a good reason: their brains are primed to learn how to navigate the social world.

Second, we can see that success with friends is not a matter of chance. There are skills we can learn to make friendships and repair them when needed.

Third, we can hold reasonable expectations for this as with any learning process: it's going to involve many mistakes, and those mistakes are essential and natural.

Let's examine some of the ways we can be helpful companions on this particular part of their adventure, the challenge of making and keeping friends.

Making Friends While Whitewater Rafting

Remember our metaphor of the whitewater river? It fits middle school in part because it represents constant change. The river is never still. You'll pass through calm water for a moment, and then the pace suddenly picks up again. So too with developmental speed in middle school. Some sixth graders seem like elementary schoolers who got off at the wrong bus stop, while others are yearning for the social complexity of middle school and ready to leap into the fray. And that young-seeming sixth grader may show up in seventh grade half a foot taller and with the beginnings of facial hair. It certainly keeps things interesting.

For us adults, it can be hard to remember what it felt like to change this much. We're in far calmer waters. We wake up each day feeling fairly similar to the day before. If we want to empathize with a middle schooler, we have to imagine what it feels like to wake up some mornings and notice that your body is literally changing shape. Or to go through a day and be shocked by the new intensity of your emotions. Or to suddenly see a friend or peer in a different light. And your friends are going through the same thing—only on a completely independent timeline as their bodies and brains mature.

Our empathy for this experience is the first step. With that sense established, here are some ways we can help middle schoolers find and keep good friends:

* **The third thing.** Face-to-face, "let's talk" style conversations are often awkward for middle schoolers. Their brains, hypersensitized to social dynamics and facial expressions in particular, have a heavy load of work to do when looking right into another person's face for an extended time, especially a peer's. *Do they hate me? Did they think that was funny? Why do they look serious all of a sudden? Should I stop talking?*

    But when they are side-by-side, maybe looking at a video together, playing a game, or working on a project, they can connect with far more ease. Remember Eric and Joaquin and how they began to connect? They didn't sit down face-to-face; they walked side-by-side, in an environment where they could observe other things going on together. That's a winning combination for most middle schoolers.

You can help these moments happen by finding activities that your child enjoys and will bring them into side-by-side contact with other kids. Just remember to give it time—this step makes friendship more likely, but we can't force it to happen on a schedule.

* **Help them build friendship skills.** At heart, friendship is about *exchange*. Friends exchange attention and interest, troubles and support, secrets and questions. The types of exchange that fuel an elementary school friendship will shift in middle school, as kids become both more sophisticated and more self-conscious. Middle schoolers can learn concrete skills to encourage a friendship, like sharing an activity together, asking questions to express interest and start a conversation, or inviting someone to join a game. They learn this best through modeling, but direct teaching plays a role as well. These skills do not need to be mysterious.

* **Expect uncertainty.** Constant change is par for the course in middle school. To avoid reacting in ways that make the challenges greater, see your child's social life as a series of experiments. They'll test identity, explore various kinds of friendships, and become members of different groups. If they share these ups and downs with you, follow the golden rule of facilitators: don't make it worse. In other words, if at all possible don't make them regret telling you by reacting strongly, blaming them, or pressuring them to respond in a particular way. Try to be a steady, warm presence during the occasional turbulence in their social lives.

* **Let them see your own social life.** You don't have to take them to coffees with friends, but if you notice that you tend to have "parent mode" and "friend mode," it's worth wondering if you can share sides of yourself that otherwise only come out with friends. Could you have a good friend over, so they can see you socializing? Or share bits of what's going on in your social life over the dinner table? Could you share some of the stories behind your friendships, especially ones that have changed over time or gone through hard patches? A light touch is advisable here, but even small moments of sharing about your social life can be helpful modeling for them.

* **If you feel the need to intervene, proceed with caution.** Banning a friend may make that person even more enticing. When it's absolutely necessary, first try to move them out of the activity where they see that friend, ideally finding new activities with different friends. Remember that your influence now is less directive and more about shaping their peer context.

* **Offer spaces to process.** As your child encounters the normal ups and downs in their social life, they may simultaneously be in the individuation process, which makes them less interested in sharing all the details with parents (if it helps, recall that this is a normal developmental phase and not a permanent state). If that's the case, they need somewhere else to turn. This is another moment where a nonparental adult—a relative, coach, mentor, etc.—or a safe space like an after-school club or an advisory program can be a profound gift to a middle schooler.

* **Make time for their social life.** This may sound obvious, but some kids' schedules are so filled that they hardly have time to be friends. Consider their personality here: for more

extroverted kids, it is likely that open, unstructured social time is ideal. For more introverted kids, unstructured social time may feel too awkward, and they may prefer activities that involve peers working on something together.

* **Be careful to separate your needs and theirs.** If a child is friendless in middle school, then it's worth taking action to help them change that, for example, by finding activities where the chances for friendship are high. But if they have at least one friend, and you find yourself wanting them to have more, be careful. You may be projecting your own needs onto them. And they may be getting to a larger social circle anyway, but at their own pace. The good news about the rapid development of middle school is that if you wait for a time, not even a long time, they will evolve and gain new capabilities and insights. Having one friend for all of sixth grade, for example, is not a bad thing. When the time is right, their social world will evolve.

Across all of these approaches, remember the developmental opportunity here. It can be upsetting, to say the least, to watch your child experience social challenges or confusion. But if they have the right supports, and assuming they aren't facing bullying, then these social efforts are exactly the right fuel for their learning. This is what the middle school brain is primed for.

When your child learns how to navigate social challenges—even simply learns that friendships can have ups and downs, and that there are tools to help—they will gain confidence and an essential set of skills for later life.

Social Media and Online Friends

Social media is a triggering topic for parents. We seem to place on it many of our fears about the world corrupting our children. This is not without reason—unprepared, unsupervised access to social media can lead to dark places—but it would be a mistake to let this fear set the tone. First because it would put us needlessly in conflict with our kids, who are likely to find social media interesting, because everything social is intensely interesting to them (and aligned with their developmental growth). Second because we would miss the opportunities included in social media.

I don't believe that social media is a negative force. It's not necessarily positive, either. It is simply a particular way of human relating, a playing field tilted in certain ways, intensifying some of our tendencies as humans. Much like we relate differently at home versus at a basketball game, each social media platform is another place in our lives, with particular rules. It happens to be a place full of people, where personal details are shared, with chances to discover new things about others, to test out identities and make new friends, all of which make it immensely appealing to our kids.

To figure out how to work with this appeal, let's first understand the rules and biases at play. Jacqueline Nesi, a leading researcher on social media and adolescents and a professor at Brown University, developed a framework of seven ways that social media changes traditional group dynamics. Based on this research, we can understand social media as:

* **Asynchronous,** which prompts adolescents to want to curate their image more, and may reduce their inhibition in conversations.

* **Permanent,** so what you say or do is recorded forever.

* **Public,** meaning you can be exposed to new people and behaviors, which has great upsides but also may lead to the contagion effect (spreading of a negative behavior) or a desire to amplify your status.

* **Available,** always on, leading to FOMO (the fear of missing out) and pressure to be responsive at all times.

* **Missing cues** that in-person connection offers, so you may not see how someone is feeling or responding, which can lead to misinterpreting their comments or to more aggression but also to greater freedom of identity.

* **Quantifiable,** particularly problematic when countable metrics are present like numbers of followers or likes, which tend to reinforce the drive for status.

* **Visual,** increasing the focus on attractiveness and on showing status symbols like expensive clothes.

So now we know how the playing field is tilted. Social media, if used without thought and care, can make our kids more status-oriented, more confused about people's reactions, and perhaps more aggressive. And yet social media also includes much of what they most want: the chance to be with peers, with relative freedom, to express themselves and see how other people express themselves. So what is a parent to do?

* **Find how to position yourself *alongside* your child.** Don't treat social media as evil, or you will simply seem out of touch or oppositional. Can you empathize with their desire to be in touch with friends or to explore what other people like or are talking about? Show your child that you understand and fundamentally agree with that impulse, even if you may disagree on how to follow it. Acknowledge if there are ways of using social media that you see as positive, like helping your child stay in touch with relatives or friends who have moved away.

* **Ask yourself if your child is getting their social needs met.** Do they have friends to hang out with at school and outside of school? Does it take a lot of effort to make this happen (like getting parents to arrange a hangout), or can they connect on their own terms, when they want (which is

one of the most attractive things about having a phone and a social media account)?

* **Don't treat all social media the same.** Different platforms and particular ways of using them can make all the difference to your child's experience. Platforms with disappearing communication or that allow anonymous interaction or ratings are more prone to abuse. Research shows that direct communication online—for example, sending direct messages—is more positive than passive scrolling and consuming of social media.

* **Prepare them for the expedition, like a guide studying the terrain.** You might look at the research together on how social media use affects adolescents, asking for their opinions and reactions as you go. You could learn together about the dangers they may encounter, from online predators to phone addiction, and discuss how to prepare for each of these. Assume that your child will have real insights to share, often from their observations of peers. If you haven't already, consider finding high-quality sex education classes for them, as viewing sexual content is almost inevitable online.

* **Establish ground rules.** With their input, you can then establish ground rules for this expedition, similar to those around a phone. This might include time limits, a "bedtime" for devices and social media apps, and agreements about what can and can't be posted. You might remind them that behavior online is treated the same way as behavior in real life. Bullying online would lead to the same consequences, for example. And because each social media platform is unique, make it clear that you need to approve each one separately, and that rules may be different for each.

* **Peer groups matter.** Hanging out with the wrong crowd online, just like in-person, can lead to bullying or the

modeling of bad behavior. But remember the other side of this coin. Finding a supportive online group can be a huge boost. I've seen students make genuine, close friendships online, discover new areas of interest, or find communities that were supportive and helpful to their growth. These don't replace the need for in-person friends, but to a middle schooler desperate to feel some sense of belonging and connection, an online social group can make all the difference, and we shouldn't undervalue it.

There is no simple rule about when kids are ready for social media. Some sixth graders have the maturity and support to handle it well; others are best served waiting until high school. But you can't avoid it forever. The chance to be liked, to connect, to discover and explore new identities—all of these are such a perfect fit for what drives adolescents. There is no stopping the draw toward social media. It's better to create healthy boundaries to channel this drive than try to stop it entirely. And as you do, make sure to consider their social needs and find ways to help them meet those in person as well.

CHAPTER SUMMARY

* Friendships are central to the happiness of just about any middle schooler, as their brain changes orient them to the social world more than anything else. Their friendship skills are growing fast, and like any busy construction site, this means that things will get messy as new skills are built. It helps to accept that social ups and downs are necessary for their learning.

* Success in friendships is mostly about skills and practice. Through modeling and teaching, we can help them learn fundamentals like the importance of shared activities or of exchanging

questions as ways to connect. We can also support them by sharing more of our own social lives and histories and making sure they have time and space to process the social bumps they experience.

* Social media is a powerful and appealing place for most tweens and teens, and it's not necessarily a bad one. To navigate it well, we need to learn its unique rules and biases. It may increase adolescents' tendencies to compare themselves and their fear of missing out but also offers ways to connect with peers and learn how others express themselves.

* With a savvy and open-minded stance toward social media, we can help our kids navigate it wisely, whether they begin using it in middle school or later. We can empathize with their desire to connect with friends online. From there, we can distinguish between different platforms, or even ways of using them, as some are healthier than others. We can create basic rules, often from looking with our child at the research, and let those rules evolve as they get older.

For Reflection

Recall a close friendship during your adolescent years. How did it begin, and how did it evolve? What did you learn through that friendship?

12

FINDING AND IMPROVING
A MIDDLE SCHOOL

In college, I hatched an audacious plan. I was going to start my own school. It would be full of adventure and meaning, an antidote to the boring, disconnected experience too many adolescents have. I worked feverishly for months on the plan, surviving good-natured attempts by friends to convince me to work on something more realistic (or better paid). I lined up every detail I could think of, and then—life happened. Plans shifted, and my school document became lost for years on an old computer hard drive.

But some dreams have a way of coming around again, and a little over a decade later, opportunity knocked. I had become a teacher, then a nonprofit director working with middle schoolers. I had begun a family and was reflecting on what I wanted to do next. While many ideas came up, I knew in my heart that the old dream to start a school was calling. It had been so long that I forgot I still had a copy of my original plan, but I stumbled upon it and updated it extensively. I then had the extraordinary luck to find a co-founder pursuing similiar ideas, and together we recruited a team of talented educators who were as passionate as we were. We set off to launch a new middle school.

Before our doors opened, we spent three years researching middle school from every angle we could imagine. We interviewed students, teachers, parents, researchers, and psychologists. We visited fascinating middle schools around the world. We went deep into the developmental research. We created partnerships with universities and professors who were delving into adolescent psychology and neuroscience. Ultimately, we came up with a design that was intended as an experiment in reimagining middle school.

As I write this, nearly another decade has passed since this project began. The school we started, Millennium School, is now a thriving middle school in San Francisco, California. It has evolved in many ways since opening, and yet the essence is the same as what we mapped out in those fruitful early years. It's a school that begins with developmental science, recognizing that middle school is a special developmental phase requiring its own approach. Building on that understanding, the school focuses on students' long-term ability to become wise, loving, and capable members of society. Much of the way we do that is by helping them have a smoother journey through adolescence, one in which they have ample time to be with friends, to process the social and emotional revelations and challenges that come, and to participate in academic projects that feel personal, social, relevant to the real world, and ultimately worth remembering.

These adventures as an educator helped me answer several questions I had in my mind. Can middle school actually be awesome? *Yes.* Can students keep their motivation and passion for learning alive during these years? Definitely *yes.* I've seen it every day, seen them ready to look adults in the eye and engage, seen them curious and sometimes frustrated but persevering as they pour their hearts into meaningful projects. We all have our checked-out days, but now I know in my bones that middle school does not need to create the stereotypical checked-out student.

Drawing on these experiences, we'll explore the question of how to find a middle school where your child can thrive. And once you find one, or one that has that potential, we'll consider how you can contribute most meaningfully as a parent. Later, in part 3, we'll look at this from an educator's perspective, examining how we can improve middle school practices from within.

Finding the Right Middle School

Sometimes parents have the luck, and challenge, to select a middle school from among several choices. For others, the question is more how to improve the middle school your child landed in. In both cases, consider the qualities below as a set of ideal elements. More are better, but we don't need all of them to make a great middle school.

1. **School culture.** School culture is the hardest element to describe clearly, but it's also the most important. One teacher may see and influence your child for an hour per day, but the school culture is teaching every single minute of every day. It teaches the school's attitude toward middle schoolers and learning in general. Are middle schoolers capable of serious work? Are multiple learning styles and personalities appreciated? Is racism or sexism embedded in the culture? Do teachers believe in social-emotional learning and have the support and time to attend to students' emotional needs?

   School culture can be felt when you walk into the building. How do students react to the adults they meet? How do they treat each other? How engaged do they seem? Is there evidence of teachers having room for creativity and playfulness in their approach? What is displayed on the walls?

   School culture has its roots in adults' mindsets. It's an expression of what the teachers and administrators believe is possible. Culture can change, but usually only slowly.

Because it has a stability to it, and also teaches more deeply than any academic subject, it's worth spending time to discover it. If you can, meet the school leader and some teachers. Are they people you'd want as a guide alongside you and your child on an adventure? Pay close attention to the attitudes of the students you interact with. Don't expect chipper elementary school attitudes, but if the tone is consistently bored or disengaged, take note.

Look for the casual interactions in particular, and take advantage of the fact that middle schoolers tend to filter adults out and focus on their friends. If you have the chance to see a less-structured, outside-of-class time like lunch, recess, or a passing period, you'll likely get a good read on the school culture.

2. **School size.** Small schools have an easier time being great schools. It's no guarantee—a big school with passionate and open-minded teachers would certainly be better than a small school with an unmotivated group of adults running it. But if you have the choice, a smaller middle school is better, and best of all would be a school of less than 150 students total.

This number is rooted in fascinating research by the British anthropologist Robin Dunbar. Based on studies of the brain size and social relationships of different primates, he theorized that human brains have, in essence, a maximum number of relationships we're wired for. His and other research suggested around 150, which has since been called Dunbar's number.

This gets interesting when applied to the size of organizations. Author Malcolm Gladwell famously told the story of the company Gore-Tex in his book *Tipping Point*, describing the company's realization that when a business unit reached more than 150 employees, social problems began to occur. Employees felt less trust and cohesion, and began to game the system, perhaps feeling less accountable to other people and more like cogs in a bigger machine. Realizing this, Gore-Tex made it a policy to create a new unit every time that number of 150 employees was reached and found that it greatly improved their culture.

Apply this to adolescents, whose social sensitivity makes them highly attuned to the peers around them, and it is not a stretch to realize that school size matters a great deal. In a small school, especially one with less than 150 students, students are more likely to feel they know the people they see. They can feel like a member of a community rather than a stranger in a crowd. Research on small schools has confirmed a wide range of benefits, from students reporting a stronger sense of connection to school, to more positive student-teacher relationships.

Think about it: if you are around strangers whose intent is unknown, how likely are you to feel open, secure, and willing to experiment to discover your authentic self, particularly in the socially sensitive middle school years? For many adolescents, a large school leads them into a kind of defensive posture, in which it feels safer to not reveal much, stay quiet, focus on a few friends, and try not to say or do anything stupid.

So while Dunbar's number is theoretical and represents a generalization, it has something to teach us about school size. At some point in size, students cease to feel connected to everyone around them and begin interpreting them as strangers. This doesn't stop a school from creating an excellent and supportive culture, but it does make the job harder. All else equal, the smaller school wins.

3. **Teaching style.** Traditional schools tend to favor one teaching style (lectures, with individual student work on worksheets and tests) and its associated learning style (being able to be quiet, sit still, and absorb information through listening). As the science of learning has progressed, we know that while this teaching style works for some, it is far from ideal for the majority of students.

What works better? We'll explore this further in part 3, but the essence is to shift from passive to active. A typical lecture invites passive listening, but a more effective learning experience invites an active response, in which students are busy creating, collaborating, brainstorming, and testing ideas. This does not mean lectures are bad, just that they need to be used in small doses.

This might mean designing classes around projects rather than units (called project-based learning). It might mean making classes interdisciplinary, for example blending English and science at times, because in life those skills are used in combination, and the combination might allow more meaningful and relevant-feeling projects. It might mean operating in student teams rather than individually, building collaboration skills and tapping into middle schoolers' natural social drive. It would surely mean less focus on memorizing bits of knowledge, many of which we have instant access to online, and instead learning the processes to guide a project or inquiry to a successful conclusion: doing research, evaluating information sources, working collaboratively, coming up with multiple potential solutions, testing ideas, and trying again.

These are all examples of teaching that draws on the science of learning. None of them individually is required for a middle school to be great. The deeper aim is to look for a teaching culture that prizes active student engagement and does not overly rely on any one method, especially traditional lectures and memorization, to get there.

4. **Perspective on social-emotional learning.** It is a rare middle school teacher who doesn't care about a child's social or emotional wellness. Teachers know that this matters immensely for student success in school. The question is really: Does the school value social and emotional wellness highly enough to make time and other resources available for it? Is there a regular advisory period? Is there training for teachers to become excellent advisors and skilled in social-emotional teaching? If a student is having a crisis, is there an adult with the time to help them? Great middle schools know that supporting personal wellness is not a luxury, it's the route toward both a happier child and better academic results.

5. **Strong advisory program.** One of the clearest ways a school can show it supports social-emotional wellness is to have a strong advisory program. Not just an advisory period, which sometimes becomes a hangout time or quiet study time, but an advisory program in which teachers, with training and support and curriculum, create space for students to talk about their emotional lives, process social situations, learn tools to manage emotions, and more. As a parent, be careful to look past the aspirational words a school may use here. Find out from teachers or students what actually goes on in a typical advisory session, how often these sessions occur, and how much support and training teachers have.

6. **Time and rituals.** Look at how time is used in a school, in the schedule and calendar, and you'll see what that school really values. Is there daily time for movement? Is there enough time to eat lunch, ideally a minimum of thirty minutes? Are classes always broken up into small chunks

of forty-five to sixty minutes, or are some extended (sometimes called a "block schedule") so that students can go
deeper into a topic? Are there regular times set aside for
community gatherings, like a morning meeting? Is the start
time aligned with the research (see chapter 9), which recommends 8:30 A.M. or later?

7. **Community involvement** There is a curious thing about
   middle schools and parent involvement. As with any school,
   an active parent base is essential to success. But unlike
   elementary kids, middle school students may not want to
   see their parents volunteering in the classroom. For all the
   developmental reasons described earlier, they are looking
   for space and the chance to develop their identity away
   from their family of origin. So what can parents do? In my
   opinion, the most powerful way for parents to volunteer is
   to become bridges between the school and the community
   around it. Instead of coming into school, find ways to bring
   the school out into the world. This might mean creating
   apprenticeships; finding field trip opportunities, perhaps to
   local businesses, artists, or others; or identifying a special
   guest speaker who can talk about their life story or their
   profession in a class.

8. **How the school assesses learning.** Traditional letter-grade
   assessment has many unintended negative consequences. It
   can feel frustratingly subjective to students. Grades alone
   lack meaningful feedback on how to grow. They are usually
   backward-looking, only talking about work that is already
   done, often without a chance to improve. Finally, they miss
   the opportunity for students to play a role in assessing their
   own work, which can build motivation and increase their
   skill in accurate self-assessment, something quite useful for
   their adult life.

For all these reasons, any time a school is working toward deeper forms of assessment, consider that a big plus. These might include a digital portfolio of student work, or the use of narratives from teachers to describe student progress, in addition to or in place of letter grades. It might include what's sometimes called "competency-based learning," in which a student works on a given skill across classes and years, not just once, and so can continue improving their score as they document more skill.

Look also for signs that students are being invited to play a role in assessing their own learning. This could be student narratives reflecting on their progress or an adaptation of the traditional parent-teacher conference into a student-led conference, in which students lead the meeting, present their work, take questions, and work with their parents and teachers to set goals.

9. **Attitude toward clubs and sports.** Back in chapter 6, we explored the essential developmental need to achieve, to feel that at least in one domain you have excellence that others notice. This is one of many reasons why the range of activities available in a middle school matters and is more than a "nice to have." Ideally, there would be enough activity options such that every student can find one area of clear success and mastery.

Do students have access to several athletic options? This doesn't mean that the school has to have its own teams in all kinds of sports—connections with local athletic leagues or youth centers also count. Are there multiple clubs available, or even the chance to create your own? Among these clubs, a signal of a positive middle school culture is the presence of an active GSA Club (Gender & Sexualities Alliance) or similar. While much depends on who is leading the club, it's extremely valuable to have space in school for students to process their questions about gender and sexuality, which are normal for this age, or to be allies for those who are asking those questions.

10. **Healthy achievement culture.** There are middle schools where the academic standards are low and students are bored, and there are middle schools that have become pressure cookers, assigning hours of homework per night and pressuring students to apply for highly selective high schools (like public magnet schools or private schools) as the only acceptable signs of success. Both of these extremes will likely have worse student mental health outcomes, among other problems.

A healthy achievement culture sets high expectations for middle schoolers, believing them capable of doing original work, presenting to real-world experts, and having a growing degree of choice in how to complete their projects. At the same time, it celebrates many forms of success and achievement and values what Stanford professor Denise Pope calls PDF—playtime, downtime, and family time—by keeping homework modest (ideally one hour or less per night, on average).

This list is more of a North Star, a set of ideals to orient toward, not a set of requirements for a great middle school. I recognize that the ability to put all these ingredients together is more likely in schools that are privileged in some way—with more money, the independence of a private school, or by serving a family population that is not struggling with basic needs. If in doubt, go back to #1: the school culture, which comes from the way adults see their work and their students, is most important. Regardless of a school's features, middle schoolers will be social sponges—they'll learn who *we* are in order to discover who *they* can be.

How Parents Can Improve Middle Schools

You've chosen or been placed in a middle school—now what? Whether to improve an already-excellent school or begin turning around a struggling one, here are some first steps to become an effective, involved parent in a middle school:

1. **Fight for teachers.** A school is not really a permanent institution—it's a temporary gathering of people who create a culture full of their ideas and mindsets. If you want to make your school better, at heart you are talking about helping the adults. That's the route toward helping our kids have better experiences.

   The first step here is to build empathy. Teachers are expected to accomplish an astonishing array of tasks, from academic growth to emotional wellness, for a group of students each bringing unique needs. They are used to constant demands and mandates; everyone from policy makers to well-meaning parents acts as if they know how to do the job better. It may also surprise you to learn that American teachers spend significantly more hours in front of students (and have less time to prepare) than teachers in many other nations, including those that often are held up as examples of excellent education systems, like Finland. On top of this, pay is low and they are given less respect than many other professions. It's a job of truly heroic proportions.

   With this empathy in your heart, come as an ally. Ask how you can help. When you make a request, coming on strong with a demand may lead to short-term action but will not build the will for lasting change. Think about how you can pair a request with resources, perhaps in the form of your own and other parents' time, connections, money raised, or invitations to be part of a peer community of

127

other teachers trying something new. Your most effective efforts will help teachers become healthier, more confident, more respected, and more prepared.

2. **Fight for the school leader** if they are someone you respect. School principal roles have a high turnover rate in many places, and this constant leadership transition creates immense challenges for schools. New principals have to take time to learn a school's routines before they become effective leaders and may launch efforts to change things but not stay long enough to see those changes through, leading teachers to ignore even well-designed reform efforts. School leaders are more likely to stay if they feel they have a strong parent base that has their back and will advocate, volunteer, and raise funds to support their initiatives.

3. **Make school a less isolated place.** Schools suffer from a tendency to become islands unto themselves, a product of the overwhelming number of mandates they're charged with, particularly the stress around high-stakes testing. Often this means that experiences like field trips, arts classes, and clubs are cut. This is not aligned with middle school development—early adolescents crave connection with the real world and need a wide range of activities to find their niche. Parents can help by creating bridges with the outside world. Help find interesting field trips if the school is open to it, and organize parent chaperones as extra support to the teachers. Offer to host a club or coach a sport. Bring an artistic talent or find others who can offer them. Help find apprenticeships and mentorships.

4. **Focus on support rather than mandates.** If you want to push for a new element in the school, say an advisory program, focus on how you can equip teachers with high-quality training, connections with a supportive peer community of other teachers, and time away from their other responsibilities to develop this new skill. If they are reluctant or resistant, don't assume that they dislike the idea. They may just be skeptical that enough time or support will be given, and like any of us, they don't want to implement a half-baked program. Unless a new school-wide mandate is absolutely essential, offer new programs or opportunities to those teachers who are already ready and excited for them. It is often more effective to have a handful of fired-up teachers testing a new concept than to get all teachers, including those actively resistant, to take on a new program.

5. **Find the low-hanging fruit.** Changing the fundamentals of a school is a multiyear effort. It's worth doing, but alongside those efforts, look for some easier wins. Small changes with big results include implementing a conflict-resolution program; offering a one-time special field trip; providing mindfulness training for interested teachers (both for themselves and to offer it to their students); creating a high-quality hangout space after school; designing a better arrival experience for new students, where they feel welcomed and have support in making new friends and navigating the school; creating ways for parents to engage and feel more expert in all things middle school, for example, with book clubs or discussion nights; and forming partnerships with local youth centers or organizations whose programs might add to the variety offered at school.

————————— CHAPTER SUMMARY —————————

* School culture matters more than how one teacher operates, more than the mission statement, more than any written curriculum. School culture is what schools really teach. You can pick it up in the casual interactions between students, in the levels of engagement you witness on a visit, and in the way teachers talk about their students. If you have a chance to select a middle school, think about culture first.

* If you have the choice, smaller schools tend to be better. Based on the fascinating research around Dunbar's number, it's reasonable to conclude that schools of 150 students or fewer will have an easier time building healthy, positive cultures.

* Beyond culture, the qualities that define an excellent middle school include an interactive teaching style; a focus on social-emotional learning; a strong advisory program; sufficient time for movement, eating, and socializing; engagement with the surrounding community; assessment that goes beyond letter grades; a diverse range of clubs and sports; and achievement expectations that believe middle schoolers can do original work without creating high stress.

* Parents can play a major role in improving a middle school. Begin by aligning yourself with the teachers—supporting their wellness and professional growth is an essential way to support your child's success. Look for ways to make schools less isolated, for example by using your network to find volunteers, guest speakers, or field trip opportunities.

* In addition to broader reform efforts, there are many small but meaningful improvements that parent volunteers can make. These range from creating a conflict-resolution program at school, to funding mindfulness trainings for teachers, to creating better arrival programs to welcome new students.

For Reflection

If you could go back and change one aspect of your middle school, something that you would remember and appreciate all these years later, what would you change?

13

TEN OPPORTUNITIES

As I write this book, a new movie has been released called *Middle School: The Worst Years of My Life*. You could fill a small library with books and films that have essentially the same title and tone. Often the most optimistic goal they suggest is simply to survive middle school. I don't doubt that the creators of these books and films are speaking from the heart, and I know that middle school is awful for so many. But the danger is that we each participate in making this nightmare come true. We see middle school as certain to be bad, we wince as our children arrive, we don't bother trying to deeply change it because somehow, we're told, these years are just rough ones and you should get through them as quickly as possible.

There's a curious bias at play here, known as *target fixation*. Reportedly, it was first identified in World War II, when American fighter pilots in training would focus so intently on attacking their target that they sometimes flew straight into it. More recent reports of this bias come from those teaching new drivers how to drive a car or motorcycle. If you tell someone to avoid a particular target, they tend to look at it, and if they aren't careful, they'll unconsciously guide their vehicle to follow their gaze. Target fixation could cause you to collide with the one thing you were trying to avoid.

I suspect this bias is at play for us parents, and for the population at large, in relating to middle school. We've heard (or remember) how bad it can be, and so avoiding those bad things often becomes our goal for our children. We don't orient as much to the opportunities of this age. Is there a better way? Could we be savvy to the pitfalls but focused on activating the incredible growth potential of these years?

We'll try to strike this balance in the chapter ahead. We'll begin with five golden opportunities: moments that you can listen for and help create, which speak to the positive potential of middle school. Then we'll explore five silver linings, each representing an area that may make us nervous as parents. Just like you might study routes up a mountain, difficult but sure to lead to a stunning view, we'll look at these as opportunities for adventure.

Golden Opportunities

1. Greater Independence

Most middle schoolers will request more independence, whether to navigate their town or city solo, to schedule time on their own with friends, or to not have you ask them about their homework. When this happens, start by giving yourself a little pat on the back. Your child is reaching toward greater autonomy in the world, just as they should be. Right on track developmentally.

But what if you think they aren't ready? If this is the case, first bring to mind the anchoring effect discussed earlier, that bias that makes us see someone (especially a child) for how they used to be, not how capable they are now. You likely will underestimate their readiness. Then, remember that your goals are aligned here. They want to be more capable in the real world, and you want them to be too. The question is just how best to get there.

The key is to place yourself alongside them. Unless the request is inappropriate for any point in life, tell them you also want them to be able to do this. Be honest about fears you have, but hold them lightly—show that you aren't certain those fears are correct. Then think together about how they could demonstrate readiness. What specific actions could they take to show you they're ready?

Here's an example. At Millennium School, we cooked up the idea of a Field Trip License. To earn it, students had to study for and pass a street smarts quiz, showing they knew how to handle various situations, like getting lost without a phone in a neighborhood they didn't know. They had to prove they had memorized the school's phone number and address. Then they received a (metaphorical) license, giving permission to attend school field trips. What equivalent could you create for your child's request? Remember that middle schoolers like to feel they are becoming more savvy and capable in the real world. Here's a chance for them to show that they can hold a responsibility and be recognized with new freedoms in proportion.

As part of this opportunity for greater independence, keep an eye out for chances to have away-from-home adventures. This could be an overnight camp, a focused program like a writer's intensive, a wilderness expedition, a Model United Nations conference, or many others. Unfortunately, money can be a barrier here, but scholarships may be available. If you or your child finds a high-quality overnight program, they may get a rare and powerful opportunity to immerse themselves in a new group and place where they can try on new roles, maybe even discover a new side of themselves.

2. Rites of Passage

Rites of passage are oddly missing from many industrialized societies—but we can create them or find places where they still exist. In chapter 14, we'll explore how rites of passage offer a sense of meaning and community support to adolescents as they go through phases of transformation. What kind of experience could you create or find for your child?

It could be a tradition you begin in your family, like a wilderness adventure at age thirteen led by a relative who loves the outdoors, in which your child gains new experiences, time with a trusted adult, and new skills and independence.

It could be a wisdom circle gathering of some kind, in which a group of close adults celebrates an adolescent at an important transition moment (like completing middle school). This group could reflect back what they see in the young person, maybe offering them a challenge or sharing some of their hard-earned wisdom on the path ahead.

It could be something you help to create at school. I know of one school where students complete a challenging and long wilderness experience, and when they return to campus, they find the entire school on the field welcoming them back and celebrating their accomplishment. What a moment that would be, a positive and lasting memory worth keeping.

Whatever form it takes, you can bring the key ingredients described in more detail in chapter 14: a community, a threshold, a ritual, and a challenge. Together these show a young person that we see and celebrate their growth. Whether it's a birthday, a graduation, a religious ceremony, or otherwise, these rites become foundation stones for an adolescent building their adult identity.

3. Voices for Justice

One of the unique and glorious things about middle school is that it takes place as students are becoming aware of the wider world and its troubles but *before* they've become jaded. Middle schoolers are just discovering the adult world, and they usually haven't accepted the injustices, paradoxes, or hiding-in-plain-sight unfairness. Thank goodness they haven't. We depend on each generation identifying some of these injustices, which we adults have come to more or less live with, and deciding that they are unacceptable. How else could we make progress?

If you hear this tone in your child, you can smile to yourself. It signifies that they are noticing more about the adult world and feeling more capable of having opinions, perhaps even trying to make changes. You don't need to push them here—that would risk making it more about you. Simply be supportive, listen and discuss when they wish, and perhaps help them discover others on a similar path. Whether it's standing up against bullying at school or fighting for longer lunch breaks, or making their opinions heard on a major issue like climate change, middle schoolers' powerful voices are worth celebrating.

4. Moments of Mastery

Sometimes, we adults miss the emerging mastery in the young people around us. We notice the habit of watching YouTube videos but neglect to realize that a hundred videos later, they are now experts on Greek mythology (as I discovered with one student I know). Or we smile knowingly at their lofty dream of becoming a rock star but don't fully appreciate that they've pushed themselves to practice singing for hours a day as a result.

At some point in middle school, your child will possess the skills to independently dig into a subject of interest, absorb skills and knowledge, create original work, and often exceed the abilities of many adults. I certainly did not understand Greek mythology as well as my student, and can only dream of being able to sing well. Middle schoolers can surpass us.

You can't force these moments of mastery or predict when they will appear, but keep an eye out. What if, in place of typical birthday or holiday presents, each year you helped them explore one topic of interest with a special lesson from an expert or a piece of equipment they need? This does not have to cost money—you can use your social network to find expertise or equipment in your local community. This is one of the ways we can best serve, by being a bridge to the wider world.

5. New Friendships

Middle school is an explosion of friend making, friend losing, grouping, and regrouping. This leads to some of adolescents' greatest challenges but also some of the sweetest victories. While we prepare to help them with social drama when it happens, we can also orient toward this potential: most middle schoolers will discover rich new friendships.

Chances are, these friendships will be closer and more intense than anything they've experienced before. They'll feel more connected to their peers and will enjoy their company even more. They'll have more complex feelings and thoughts to exchange. They'll have secrets to share and inside jokes to savor. For all that middle school is known for social drama, remember that it's because adolescents are deeply driven to find friendships and have rapidly growing skills to understand the social world.

We can support these efforts by accepting that social ups and downs are normal, teaching and modeling friendship skills, and helping youth find spaces to process their social questions. Then you can celebrate and enjoy their steps toward one of the greatest joys humans can experience: friendship.

Challenges with a Silver Lining

The following are five more opportunities for growth, but each begins with something that parents often dread. We'll try to tunnel under the issue to find the fundamental developmental needs at play. Then you can position yourself alongside your child, helping them meet those needs in healthy ways, and perhaps even finding the silver lining of each challenge as you do.

1. Phones

The challenge: "All of my friends already have a phone!" is the classic line, accompanying an urgent request for their own device. Many of us parents immediately assume a defensive posture, imagining the ways our children will become addicted to the phone or wander into the darkest corners of the internet.

Their developmental needs: *I want a phone* likely means *I want to connect with my friends* or *I want to belong and it seems like phones help that a lot.* Remember that whatever brings them into better contact with peers, they want, and they're primed for the valuable learning that results. You could also translate their request as *I'm older now and a phone represents being independent.*

How we can guide them through:

* **Be fellow researchers.** Read articles together on phone addiction, body image issues related to social media, or tips on how to use phones wisely. Let them also teach you based on how they've seen peers succeed or struggle.

* **Set agreements.** These might include a "bedtime" for the phone, time limits for use each day, rules about parents' rights to see what's on their child's phone, or the use of internet filters.

* **Join them.** Let's be honest—adolescents are not the only ones prone to phone addiction. If you feel your relationship with your phone is less than ideal, consider setting your own personal goal as part of this plan, like limiting your hours of use, so that they see you working on your skills openly as well.

* **Talk about pornography.** Even if you take great care, the difficult truth is that many middle schoolers using phones or other devices will stumble upon or find pornography. This is another reason to make sure they have access to an

excellent sex education program, ideally before *and* during middle school. The program should include frank talk about the stereotypes and negative messages conveyed in pornography, as well as safe space for adolescents to ask questions and get factual, non-shaming answers.

* **Phone or no phone, make sure their developmental needs are met.** If you determine that they are not yet ready for a phone, focus on how else you can help them meet their social needs or the drive for independence. That is what's really at stake. This might mean helping them connect with friends or schedule time together without going through parents (as this is one of the biggest advantages of a phone) or giving them degrees of greater independence in other ways, like getting themselves to school or to friends' houses.

The silver lining: Whether in sixth grade or not until high school, let's assume that sooner or later, after thoughtful consideration and clear agreement making, you give your child access to a phone. They now have the chance to make a leap in independence. As they seem ready, you can begin granting them more freedom of movement, knowing you can check in. You can ask them to pick things up on the way home. They can schedule their own time with friends. You can meet their need to have more autonomy, thanks to this magical communications technology. And, while complex and scary, the online world they'll begin accessing more is one they have to learn to navigate skillfully. It's fundamental to their long-term success.

2. Video Games

The challenge: As much as social media, video games have the ability to grab and hold an adolescent's attention and, at the same time, deeply disturb their parents. We may worry about addiction, exposure to violence, or the sheer time taken away from other valuable activities.

Their developmental needs: Video games tap into at least two key developmental drives. The first is social: a game may be played with others online, and even if not, it may be part of the daily conversation at school, offering an easy way to connect with friends. Second, video games tap into the enjoyment of competition. In fact, they offer some of the most satisfying experiences of competition out there, demonstrating how well-designed competitions can motivate us: each player consents to compete, experiences objective rules, gets regular feedback on how they're doing, and witnesses their practice leading to better results.

How we can guide them through:

* **Work on the needs first.** Before we directly address video games themselves, is your child getting their social and competitive needs met elsewhere? Just as social media can go badly for a middle schooler if it's their only social outlet, if video games are their only way to experience the thrill of competition, they're more at risk of developing an unhealthy relationship to them. Consider if there are also offline ways to help them enjoy connection and competition, anything from a sports team to a Dungeons & Dragons club.

* **Create agreements together.** As with phones and social media, take the spirit of looking at the research together, expecting your child to have valuable insights (from personal experience and observing peers) and trusting them to help you shape agreements. These might include time limits, a balance of video game time with other in-person forms of competition, or the use of the video game rating system.

* **Keep a balanced view on video game violence.** While the violence in video games can be off-putting, and may be cause for alarm if you detect more aggressive behaviors that

seem to relate to it, for most kids there does not seem to be reason for major concern. This has been a hotly debated question in psychology research, but many recent studies have found no correlation between video game use and aggression. The case is not closed, as some research has had other results. But in my experience, most middle schoolers are easily able to tell the difference between video game violence and real-world behaviors. If they are playing video games in moderate amounts and have other forms of real-life social time and competition in their lives, then in most cases they can enjoy gaming in a healthy way.

The silver lining: Just as we adults might enjoy a poker night with friends, both as a break from daily responsibilities and for the fun of the game, adolescents find many of the same pleasures in video games. In addition to being social and offering satisfying competition, video games are also an ideal third thing, or a shared point of focus that makes social connection easier and less stressful. This explains part of their appeal to middle schoolers—but it also opens a door for you as an adult. If there are opportunities to game *with* your child, you might discover a new way to connect, a third thing to talk about and bond over. And you just might enjoy the game too.

3. Focus and Forgetfulness

The challenge: Middle schoolers are famous for their distractibility and difficulties with organization. Your child may forget assignments, lose materials, or allow their backpack to degenerate into a primordial soup.

Their developmental needs: This challenge is not because anything is wrong with them—in fact, far from it. It's that they are being asked to make huge leaps in complexity, shifting to multiple teachers and classes per day and more elaborate homework and projects, not to mention more intense social dynamics. Their brains are working overtime to adapt to these new realities. Developmentally, they may still be in what psychologist Jean Piaget termed the "concrete" stage, in which they orient more toward tasks right in front of them and might not appreciate something more abstract, like a social studies project due in a month's time. During middle school they'll work through this and become more skilled in abstract thinking and planning tasks, but most will need support to make this transition.

How we can guide them through:

* **Remember that this is temporary.** Their lives are complicated and full of change. Their brains are evolving rapidly toward greater ability for abstraction and focus. Begin with empathy, and trust that with support and practice, they will get there.

* **Offer concrete tools:** Organization challenges are greatest when a child is still a concrete thinker but is being given complex and abstract tasks. We can help them by providing tools that make those abstract tasks more concrete. For example, say they have a big project due in a month. We can offer a visual planner, tactics like breaking it down into a series of steps, and the approach of blocking time on their calendar for each step. We can also help them establish consistent routines, such as a particular hour for homework or rules like homework before screen time. Quick check-ins with an adult as part of that sequence are useful, too, and by agreeing in advance can feel like part of the routine rather than interruptions from a nosy parent.

* **Keep their physical needs in mind.** We all are more attuned to certain senses than others. Understanding your child's unique sensory profile, as we explored in Chapter 9, can help you set up an ideal study space or suggest effective methods for them to regain calm and focus. Keep their

need for movement in mind as well—if they've been largely seated and still during the school day, they may need active time before doing homework. Finally, remember that exercises with cognitive complexity—where you have to concentrate and think strategically as you move—have the biggest impact on focus skills.

* **Teach mindfulness.** Mindfulness helps us grow in many ways, and it starts by developing the ability to calm and clear our minds. There are many wonderful books, classes, videos, and apps to teach mindfulness to adolescents. This may also make for an ideal shared learning experience, as most of us adults could benefit from greater mindfulness skills as well.

The silver lining: Adolescents are leaping and tumbling into their adult brain and body. When we help them develop tools for focus and organization, we're adding essential equipment to their new, more powerful brains. Keep in mind that the habits built in adolescence have particularly lasting influence. Whether it's the way they use a planner, the skills to break projects down into component parts, or mindfulness tools to focus their attention, these habits of mind will be fundamental building blocks for a productive and peaceful adult life.

4. Dating and Sexuality

The challenge: It's hard to predict just when, but sooner or later most adolescents will tune in to the social dynamic of dating, experience romantic interest, and begin to reckon with their sexual curiosity and desires. Chances are it will open up new identity questions, add intensity to their social lives, and stir up fears in the adults around them.

Their developmental needs: We know that middle schoolers are highly motivated to understand the social world—and at some point, whether in middle school or after, that social world will include romantic relationships. Meanwhile, as puberty progresses and they become aware of their own sexuality, they'll become exceedingly curious about what's OK and not OK and what's "normal." Confusion and shame easily emerge. They need accurate information and supportive, accepting guidance from adults.

How we can guide them through:

* **Be careful about jumping to conclusions.** Sometimes a sixth grader who declares that they have a boyfriend may mean something quite different from what adults imagine. It's easy to inadvertently project our adult view of dating and relationships onto them. Go in with a spirit of curiosity, learning what you can about their experience.

* **Stay open-minded with their identity experiments.** It's common for middle schoolers to question elements of their identity around gender and sexual orientation. They may try on many identities as they seek what is authentic to them. They deserve to be taken seriously, as this is an age of discoveries about who you are—and at the same time we should understand that their identity is often experimental and may or may not be permanent. The more we stay calm and open-minded, showing that our love is not conditional, the more middle schoolers will be able to try on different identities to see which fit, and the more they'll do that publicly rather than in secret.

* **Remember how intense it is for them.** Middle schoolers begin to experience the kinds of situations that can be traumatic for adults, like a breakup, but without the years of experience we adults have to temper our emotions. It's likely to be an intense ride. Try not to downplay their emotions, though you can help to normalize that, for nearly all

of us, failed relationships teach us over time how to create better ones.

* **Use the power of the third thing.** Having a shared focus, instead of a face-to-face conversation, can lower anxiety and invite more open dialogue. This is true for sensitive questions about dating or sexuality as well. Look for opportunities where a show, movie, or situation in the news speaks about relationships and sexuality—it won't be hard to find—and use that as a jumping-off point for conversation.

* **Find a good health and sexuality program.** It's so important that middle schoolers have access to good sex ed—and, unfortunately, most schools do not have good sex ed. You may need to find this elsewhere. Ideally beginning before middle school, they need access to honest, accurate information about sexuality and relationships, clear teaching around the principle of consent, and the chance to ask the questions they really want to ask (often anonymously). The key ingredient is an adult who can talk about sexuality factually and without shame or judgment.

* **Know your limits.** If you are comfortable talking with your child about dating and sexuality, it can open an important channel of communication and normalize these questions. But at the same time, if you've gone as far as you can and find yourself becoming too uncomfortable or unsure in these conversations, don't beat yourself up about it. Your job is to make sure they have someone to talk about these topics, not to always be the one to do it.

* **Make books and resources available.** If possible, make sure they have access to well-presented, factual information about dating and sexuality. I know many parents who buy or borrow a handful of age-appropriate books on health and sexuality and simply leave them in their child's room. There

are also excellent websites (like www.amaze.org), podcasts, YouTube videos, and other sources to offer.

* **Remember that friendship skills are the basis for healthy romantic relationships.** Whether through family modeling and conversations, social-emotional learning programs, or elsewhere, teaching your child fundamental friendship skills will support them when it's time to experiment with dating. The tools for self-awareness, healthy boundaries, good listening, empathy, and more will make a strong foundation.

The silver lining: When I ask parents to describe their long-term hopes for their child, one of the most consistent answers I hear is that their children will one day find happy, long-term romantic partnerships. There's the opportunity. If we can support them when they're ready to begin exploring relationships and sexuality—with our own open-mindedness and through excellent programs and resources we identify—then we help them build the skills to one day have satisfying, lasting partnerships. There aren't many goals more worthy than that.

5. Staying Connected

The challenge: It's so common as to be cliché: the middle schooler who can't stand to talk to their parents, who finds their every question or behavior intensely aggravating, and whose life seems to become more of a black box by the day. It may be one of our greatest fears as parents.

Their developmental needs: In chapter 2 we explored the healthy developmental process called individuation, which is nothing less than the making of an individual. It involves an adolescent creating more separation from their family of origin as they look to define themselves in the wider world, particularly the world of peers. As painful as it can be, it also represents a wise investment of their energy: they're working hard to understand their peer world, which will be the heart of their social life, the key to their success in careers and more. Remember also that their brains are changing to orient them intensely toward the world of peers. Developmentally, if both peers and parents are available, they can't help but focus on the peers.

How we can guide them through:

* **Change roles.** We have a chance to try on a new role, shifting from the boss of a younger child to a companion of an adolescent. In some ways, this entire book is the story of how to make this transformational change. It's not easy, but it will reveal far more of the magic of this age and open new ways to be a connected and helpful companion to your child.

* **If they seem resistant or uninterested in a question, drop it.** Would you bother a friend with the same question again and again if they never seemed to want to answer? Questions that are too direct, or that require them to summarize their day or a given experience, often feel boring or frustrating for middle schoolers. We can do better.

* **Comment on things together.** Be side-by-side with them, both literally and metaphorically, looking at something together. That might be a movie, a situation in the world, a project, a comic strip, or the passing sights of a walk.

* **Share a hobby.** This could be in an area of your interest or, better yet, by finding interest in one of their hobbies. What if they taught you how to play Minecraft? Such adventures are likely to be humbling in the best way.

* **Find space to connect when peers aren't around.** If a peer is even potentially within sight or earshot, they are likely to be drawn toward them, distracted by them, and not sure if

your presence is embarrassing. When you have the chance for time with them away from peers, whether it's a walk to the store or a short trip or a shared hobby in the garage, they can show you their more sincere side.

* **Offer chances for them to show their maturity and responsibility.** Remember, when you align yourself with one of their developmental drives, you'll have their full attention. When you speak more openly about a personal conflict or a difficult social moment, you are showing that you trust them and see them as a thoughtful conversation partner (of course, not all adult difficulties should be shared with middle schoolers in the name of connection—the point is just to share more than you used to, to honor their growing maturity). If you are helping them gain more independence, or asking them for input into a family decision, they are likely to receive this as a vote of confidence and a reason to engage.

* **Rediscover your own interests and passions.** As author Michelle Icard writes, "If your kid senses that you or your happiness depends too much on him, he may begin to pull away." This is yet another reason why parenting a middle schooler is an invitation to rediscover your interests and passions and hobbies. They need to see fully alive adults engaged with the world: that means you.

The silver lining: The opportunity here is as immense as the fears this challenge brings up. If we want to stay connected as our children evolve, we must *evolve with them.* You can rediscover your own interests, accept more of your quirks, and reveal more of your inner world. You can release some of the responsibility to control them. You can give them more freedom and responsibility and, with patience and support, watch them gradually gain the skills to hold it well. You can borrow one of the best parts of adolescence, the spirit of growth and possibility, and let it reenergize your personal growth. If you do, you can maintain much of your connection with them (not all—remember that they need to grow beyond their family of origin) *and* prime the relationship for renewed connection in their twenties, on the new basis of being fellow adults in the world together.

─────────── CHAPTER SUMMARY ───────────

* The middle school years are not just a series of dangers to be navigated. They contain some of the most profound leaps in understanding and sophistication of our whole lives. As much as we prepare for the potential challenges, we should spend at least as much energy activating the opportunities of this age.

* We explored five golden opportunities, each a signal of your child's growing skill and understanding: offering greater independence; finding or creating rites of passage; appreciating middle schoolers' natural orientation toward justice; helping them find clear mastery in at least one area; and supporting the creation of new and deeper friendships.

* Middle school also has its share of pitfalls, as is all too well known. Underneath each of these challenges there are deep developmental needs at play. Understanding those needs offers us a way out of potential conflict, as we can help our children meet their developmental needs in healthy and positive ways.

* We explored five challenges: phones; video games; struggles with focus and forgetfulness; dating and sexuality; and the challenge to stay connected with your child during adolescence.

For Reflection

Of the various middle school dilemmas you faced—perhaps to do with social life, your family, academics, your identity, or otherwise—can you think of one in which an adult responded with real wisdom and support? How did they do it? And can you think of one where adults failed to respond well—what do you wish could have been the response?

BEYOND SCHOOL

If you've read this far, you know that middle schools can be magical. They can be places where young people feel safe and connected, where they're engaged in deep projects that have real-world impact, and where they can make sense of the social-emotional turbulence of adolescence.

But even the best middle schools can't do everything. There will always be some magic beyond their reach, whether it's a life-changing relationship with a mentor, a passion project like learning how to cook well, or the experience of becoming an activist for a cause. Any one of these experiences could make a profound difference in a middle schooler's life. What would happen if we thought as carefully about these beyond-school experiences as we did with all that happens in the school day?

This is not to downplay academics—but we have to turn to the other pages of the menu, too. What about the experience of writing a letter of forgiveness or gratitude? Or completing a rite of passage on an extended wilderness trip? Or apprenticing yourself to an adult to explore a personal interest? In this chapter we'll explore these beyond-school experiences. Each represents a way to help middle schoolers discover who they are, how to connect, and how to contribute to the world.

The Essential Experiences Project

For years now, I have been asking people of all ages what was the most essential part of their middle school journey. I've asked current and recently graduated middle schoolers, high schoolers, and adults. The point is not to come up with "the answer" to this question, which is going to be different for each person. The point is to invite us all to ask this question, to wonder about the answers, and to keep orienting toward the experiences that come up.

The list below represents the answers that have come up repeatedly. Each is framed as a personal challenge. Sometimes I can't help but wonder: What if these were the primary curriculum of middle school?

1. Apprentice yourself to someone.
2. Ask an unanswerable big question.
3. Ask for honest feedback.
4. Become a changemaker.
5. Become a great question asker.
6. Become a pen pal.
7. Become friends with someone over seventy-five.
8. Break a stereotype.
9. Care for an infant.
10. Celebrate a personal failure.
11. Challenge a limiting belief.
12. Change one habit to help the Earth.
13. Connect with your lineage.

14. Create a healthy habit.

15. Create an original work of art.

16. Create your own constellation in the night sky.

17. Cross a social boundary.

18. Dance in the rain with a friend.

19. Deconstruct an advertisement.

20. Design and build something from scratch.

21. Discover bias in your thinking.

22. Discover your privilege.

23. Do daily random acts of kindness.

24. Express your gratitude.

25. Figure out your strengths.

26. Find a mentor.

27. Find an awe spot in nature.

28. Forgive someone.

29. Give feedback to authority.

30. Grow an edible plant from seed.

31. Join a political campaign.

32. Join a team.

33. Keep a journal.

34. Lead a group.

35. Learn a new language.

36. Learn about an unfamiliar religion.

37. Learn how to be an active listener.

38. Learn how to calm yourself.

39. Make a new friend.

40. Make a vision board.

41. Mediate a peer conflict.

42. Open a bank account.

43. Practice mindfulness every day.

44. Serve a good meal.

45. Set a boundary with someone.

46. Sing under a bridge.

47. Speak an uncomfortable truth.

48. Spend time in a group where you stick out.

49. Stand up for someone.

50. Start a business.

51. Take public transit independently.

52. Train for a new physical skill.

53. Tutor someone.

54. Walk more than five miles in a day.

55. Write a personal credo.

As you read this list, what would you add to it from your own journey?

Perhaps you're noticing the links between these experiences and middle schoolers' developmental tasks. Need to break out of the Belonging stage? How about #17, crossing a social boundary, or #8, breaking a stereotype. Need to feel more confident in your ability to achieve? How about #53, tutoring someone, or #52, training for a new physical skill?

I have seen students and adults offer these challenges to each other or take the same one on together. I've seen students design board games with these challenges laid out like Monopoly tiles, rolling the dice to see where they would land. I've seen students simply read through the list and then narrow it down to one that speaks most to them, sometimes to do solo, sometimes to undertake with a supportive group in which every student chooses one. And I've seen adults keep these in their metaphorical back pocket as fodder for conversations or mentorship.

However you use these, I suggest you keep it playful, not another curriculum sequence but more like a choose-your-own adventure book. Just one of these, offered at the right time and received in the right way, can be life changing. Here's a story from one middle schooler, whose adventure of taking public transit independently (#51) left a lasting impression.

*

I was about a month into middle school and I had been going to school on the train with my mom or dad. By then I knew the route by heart and felt confident enough to do it independently. My parents agreed that I was experienced enough, so one morning they finally let me try taking the train alone. I left the house at around 7:30, even though my school started at 8:30 and the trip only takes twenty-five minutes. As I walked down the hill to the train station all I could think about were the worst-case scenarios. What if I get mugged? What if I get lost? What if I'm late to school? I got to the station and almost as soon as I hit the stairs a train pulled in.

I speed walked, trying not to draw too much attention to myself. I stopped at where I usually got on with my parents and waited for the train to pull up. The doors opened and I took an open seat. There was a person muttering to themselves and pacing up and down the train. I lowered my head and averted my eyes. They aren't going to do anything to you, I thought to myself, all is good. At the next stop the train starts to get crowded. I am jostled a little bit as the train starts down the tracks. At the second-to-last stop, a woman gets on the train with her dog. Seeing the dog made me happier, and this is when I started to focus on the positive. I'm most certainly on time (the time is 7:45), I have a seat, I'm getting off next. I hop off the train and ride the escalator into the world of traffic, tent cities, and grumpy people. I walk past garbage cans that smell disgusting, people sleeping on sidewalks, and cars honking at each other. I walk down the hill to my school, and nothing bad happens. As I walk into the doors of school I think, That went great! Nothing bad happened!

Now that I have traveled independently, it feels like there is so much more to explore. I'm not confined to traveling with my parents, and I can do more on weekends and with friends. For example, over the summer my cousin and I took the train around the city and explored different neighborhoods. Now I usually go to school on my own, have gone to see friends on my own, and can unveil more layers of my city and myself.

✳

This experience was over and done within an hour, but its effect will be long-lasting. This student had opened up the city he lived in. He was discovering more of what he could do in the world and developing an identity as someone with the skills and savvy to navigate it well. These are the kind of outcomes possible, of course with good preparation and suport, when young people embark on these and other essential experiences.

Apprenticeships

One of the experiences on the list above is particularly close to my heart: apprenticeships. Perhaps it's because apprenticeships are the oldest play in the educational book. After all, long before the advent of public schooling, skills were often passed down from an adult to a younger apprentice. It taps into many of the most fundamental and effective ways we learn: one-on-one, knowledge sent on the carrier signal of a relationship, learning happening in the course of working on something together, getting feedback, and trying again. It lines up beautifully with the developmental drives in middle school, particularly the desire to contribute and to have exposure to real-world adults and issues.

These days, apprenticeship may bring to mind learning a trade like plumbing, and that's where it is still most commonly used, to great effect. But it does not need to be limited to the trades. The fundamentals work well in nearly any field, and can provide some of the most memorable and empowering learning experiences in a middle schooler's life.

I feel confident saying this because I spent ten years creating apprenticeships for middle schoolers through a nonprofit I co-founded, Spark (www.sparkprogram.org). Spark has grown into a national program serving thousands of middle schoolers, with the aim of using apprenticeships to restore their love of learning and increase their success in school. The stories generated are enough to fill many books: I've seen middle schoolers produce music in professional recording studios, code software, help design buildings, and much, much more.

Perhaps the most surprising thing about apprenticeships is how available they are, if only you ask. I will never forget the experience of trying to find the first set of apprenticeships, when the program was brand-new and my co-founder and I, both barely out of college, were making everything up as we went. One of our first students, a tall, quiet boy named Taril, had made an earnest request: he wanted to apprentice with a pilot and learn how to fly a plane.

I remember trying to lower his expectations, thinking that this was a near impossibility. Who was going to let a twelve-year-old into a cockpit? It took me some time to work up the courage to start calling around, beginning with a local flight school I had found online.

I nervously dialed the flight school, and soon was connected with a flight instructor. I explained the idea of an apprenticeship, and that it was this boy's dream to learn to fly. *Would you consider taking him on as apprentice?* To my shock, then and to this day, the answer to that first call was yes. For this man, who loved flying and loved teaching, it sounded like a pleasure. He agreed on the spot. We introduced him to Taril, and after the paperwork and preparation, their work began in earnest. Taril described what happened next:

I was surprised when my Spark coordinator told me that I would actually be flying a real plane. They hooked me up with a mentor and I thought he was the best mentor ever. His name is Dave and he taught me various things about the structure of planes, the mechanics needed to make a plane fly, and important information about how I can make my dream to be a pilot be a reality. I spent up to two hours per day with Dave for the first week, going over everything about flying and airplanes. When he first let me be the pilot, I was so excited. I couldn't believe I was actually doing it on my own. With Dave guiding me step by step, I took off, flew, and landed the plane. It was an awesome feeling and made me seriously think about the idea of being a pilot in the future. Nothing beats the rush when I was among the clouds and looking down at the land below. The earth looks awesome from above, and I felt like I was a king rising above in the clouds mastering my ship.

*

I was there that day, standing beside the runway of the small local airport, my heart swelling with pride. One boy's request had gone from an impossibility to an unforgettable experience, just by asking. I learned then that apprenticeships are powerful for middle schoolers, and that they are available. And I learned how valuable they are for the adults too. For the mentor, sharing their skill and passion with a motivated apprentice is a pleasure and even a joy. If you're curious about how to create an apprenticeship, see Appendix 2 for some tips.

Facilitated Peer Groups

Among the most powerful beyond-school experiences for middle schoolers is the chance to be in a safe, honest group of peers, where they can talk about what is most on their minds. A space to make sense of adolescence together. This might mean wondering about friendships or how to make conversation, handling sibling conflict or school stress, learning how to resolve conflicts, challenging each other to get over a limiting belief, or more. Ideally, these groups are small—eight to twelve middle schoolers—and led by an adult who creates a feeling of safety, models openness and warmth, and balances raising planned topics with listening to see which topics are emerging naturally.

In some schools this is what advisory is, and the students in those schools are lucky indeed. (In chapter 16, we explore how to create this kind of program in a middle school.) For students who are not able to find groups like this in school, there may be beyond-school ways to experience this kind of support. I've had the chance to contribute to one such project, Argonaut (www.argonaut.school), and of course I'm biased as a result.

Argonaut creates peer groups of middle schoolers who meet online, with a facilitator, after school. Over the course of a year together, they form friendships across distance, even across countries and continents, as they build trust, share what's happening in their lives, learn social-emotional tools together, and support each other through the adventure of adolescence.

There are other groups like this as well, and with luck the field will grow. There are mentoring circles operated by youth centers, faith organizations, or wilderness education groups. Sometimes a Scout group, when led by someone with the skills for facilitating these honest conversations, offers this spirit. Wherever you can find it, it is a precious gift to offer. Imagine if you had such a group when you were twelve and could speak authentically, ask the most important questions on your mind, and hear what your peers honestly thought about, well, everything, in a safe and supportive space. It's a resource worth searching hard to find.

Rites of Passage

There is one final category of beyond-school experience worth exploring here: rites of passage. A rite of passage is an experience that helps someone mark a transition from one phase of life into another. Done well, they help us find meaning in the major changes in our lives. They bring community together to celebrate and even sanctify these moments. Think of a wedding, one of the most important rites of passage in many cultures, in which two people's relationship is celebrated and affirmed by a community, rituals are completed, and a clear marker of before and after is established, signified in language (terms like "husband" and "wife"), in items (wedding rings), in legal status, and more.

Yet while weddings or the Jewish tradition of bar and bat mitzvahs are vibrant examples of rites of passage, there are precious few others in many modern, industrialized countries like the United States. Or, perhaps more accurately, there are precious few *intentional* rites of passage, where people purposefully gather to celebrate and convey new responsibilities and freedoms. We seem to have lost these in the course of modernization, particularly for youth, and so in their place we have many unintentional rites of passage. Many of these take place in high school or college: Getting your driver's license. Drinking alcohol. Having your first serious romantic relationship. Getting a job. These can each be important moments or not, positive or negative or even traumatic, but they are missing something essential.

Young people, particularly adolescents with their rapid evolution toward adulthood, need the wisdom of a community to help them make meaning out of the head-spinning changes they're going through. Instead of feeling that the adults resist them, or perhaps are baffled and annoyed by them, they need to feel that adults understand these changes, celebrate them, give them meaningful challenges to show how they've grown, and then convey new levels of freedom and responsibility.

To give one example, I've heard too many stories of young people who were never given guidance or even a heads-up before their first menstrual period, and for whom this rite of passage was barely celebrated, perhaps discussed briefly and awkwardly, or even actively hushed up. What if moments like this were instead honored, perhaps with different generations coming together, welcoming a young person into their circle, answering their questions, sharing stories, and celebrating them for the changes they're experiencing? In the first version you have a confused adolescent trying to make sense of their changing body largely on their own; in the second you have a proud adolescent realizing that they're on a journey of transformation, surrounded by wise and affirming companions.

Another clear opportunity for a rite of passage is a graduation, celebrating the completion of one stage of education. Here we do have customary ceremonies, but too often they are lackluster and impersonal, a quick walk across the stage to get a diploma. At Millennium School, when it was time for our first graduation ceremony, we attempted to create something more meaningful, and even beyond our own efforts, we discovered that students could play the key role in creating a beautiful rite of passage.

It began something like this: we dedicated the last week of eighth grade to a weeklong wilderness expedition. Students had been building up to this over the full three years of middle school, with prior camping and hiking trips developing their skills and comfort in the outdoors. For this trip, we had prepared a little surprise. On the second to last day, we embarked on a mountain hike high in the Sierra Nevada mountains, in a magical early-June landscape in which snow was still covering the ground yet the air was warm enough for short sleeves. The snow was melting into streams, pouring into a high mountain lake.

We climbed up and over boulders, and made our way to a high lookout point. Then we invited each student to find a sit spot, a quiet place just for themselves, alone with their journals. They were making some notes about what was changing for them, what it felt like to be at this moment in their lives. As they wrote, their advisors— the teacher they had known best over the past three years—were opening a box of top-secret letters, written by the students' parents without their knowledge. These were letters of recognition: parents saying what they saw in their children, what amazed them, how they were witnessing growth and transformation, and how proud they were of them.

The advisors clambered over the boulders and delivered these letters one at a time to their advisees. Surprised students opened the letters, reading them quietly in the stunning landscape, most of them with tears streaming down their faces. After some time to absorb this alone, we gathered in a lookout spot and invited students to speak out what they were experiencing, and how they saw this moment of transition in their lives. It was a powerful moment. There was a quiet sense that something important was happening, a graduation more meaningful than walking across a stage. But it was their turn to surprise us next.

As we began hiking down the mountain a short while later, we took a new path and soon came to an impasse. The melting snow had turned a stream into a mini-whitewater river, not deep but shatteringly cold, moving fast, and perhaps twelve feet across. Students gathered on one side, and then a proposal came from one of them: What if we made this river crossing our graduation? What if we said we were eighth graders on this side and ninth graders when we got to the other?

It took us a moment, but then we adults in the group recognized that something important was happening. The students were spontaneously inventing their own rite of passage. Watching them, I felt proud of their ability to turn an ordinary moment, even a potentially difficult one, into something meaningful and maybe even unforgettable. One teacher volunteered to stand in the middle of this mini river, freezing his own feet to serve as a support halfway through the crossing.

One at a time, on the eighth-grade shore, students took off their hiking boots, swinging them over their shoulders on tied shoelaces, and set foot gingerly into the near-freezing water. When they reached the center, they paused to shake hands with the teacher there, who invited them to hold an intention or at minimum to pause and notice the experience they were having. Then they walked across, to whooping and hollering and cheering from all involved, and they became ninth graders. All knew this meant leaving our community. One at a time we adults watched them go, tears in our own eyes.

Two days later they walked across an auditorium stage and picked up diplomas, in what was also a beautiful ceremony—but in my heart it was the river crossing that was the real rite of passage.

I tell this story to show that we can create these missing rites of passage in our lives. The ingredients are simple. First, a *community*: people you trust, who can witness and celebrate you. Second, a *threshold*: something that marks the transition between two places or phases. Ideally this is a physical marker, like the river in the graduation story. Third, a *ritual*: in our graduation ceremony, the rituals were the surprise letters, the student circle in the clearing, and finally the crossing of the river with a handshake in the center. Fourth, a *challenge*: something that requires a slight risk or push out of your comfort zone. This might be the push to speak in front of a group or to set foot in a freezing stream. It adds emotional depth and a reminder that you can do hard things.

Taken together, these ingredients offer the power to help adolescents notice what is happening in themselves and others, celebrate change, and make a lasting memory that will influence and inspire them in the future. The drive for these climactic moments is deep and developmental. Young people will always seek rites of passage—it's up to us to help create the most meaningful, positive, and connective of rites.

What's Possible

Imagine your child or student completing eighth grade, looking forward to high school, able to reflect back on experiences like these.

They've apprenticed with a blacksmith and a computer programmer. They've done a seven-day wilderness expedition and learned to set up their own camp. They've gained and lost friends, learned some ways to resolve conflicts, and become confident that they can make new friends in high school. They've been celebrated in personal, powerful ways by the peers and mentors closest to them on their completion of middle school. They have seen that they can be socially and emotionally savvy, capable in the world, able to grow. These are each parts of their identity clicking into place. These are middle school graduates ready to take on the world, to thrive in a wide range of high schools and beyond, with their motivation, engagement, and authentic voice still intact.

Much of our job as adults is to help them find these essential developmental experiences, trusting those experiences in turn to evoke the skills and insights that are waiting to emerge.

CHAPTER SUMMARY

* Many of the most profound growth experiences for middle schoolers will take place outside of school. What if we explored and mapped these as carefully as we did any academic area?

* By asking each other about which experiences were most essential and positive in middle school, we'll keep generating interesting ideas, whether it's the challenge to write an original song or to start a business, or many more. We can offer these as challenges to each other, between adults and young people, or in games, as ways to prompt the deep learning possible beyond school.

* Apprenticeships are a timeless and powerful way to gain both skills and confidence, and they are more available to middle schoolers than we might think.

* Advisory-like spaces such as Argonaut groups offer a safe space for middle schoolers to share what's on their minds and hearts, gain social-emotional tools when they're most needed, and make sense of their adolescent adventures together. In an ideal world, every young person would have access to such a group.

* Intentional rites of passage are often missing for our young people today, but we have the ability to create them. We can blend the ingredients of community, a threshold, a ritual, and a challenge together to make unforgettable moments that give meaning to a middle schooler's journey of transformation.

For Reflection

What were the most powerful, positive learning experiences you had outside of school at this age? What rites of passage have you participated in? What could you imagine creating for the middle schoolers in your life to mark an important moment of transition?

PART 3

TEACHING TRANSFORMATION

In my first months as a school leader, in charge of a brand-new school I had co-designed, I ended each day in a very small office shared with four other educators. It was so tiny that for any given meeting someone would be on the floor, someone sat on a table or bookshelf, and a lucky few had chairs. Our small team huddled together like sailors in a storm, trying to read the waves, plot our course, and figure out how to keep the ship together.

Like other educators starting new school models, we were doing something risky and a bit audacious—creating a school unlike anything we had experienced ourselves. We could not rely on any memory of what this was supposed to be like. We would have to experiment, continually sense what was working and not, and change as we go. Transformation was all around us. We were changing as educators, our school model was changing, and the students we served were changing most dramatically of all.

Luckily, we were not as alone as our tiny office sometimes felt. Other educators on this path, founding teams at innovative schools around the United States and in other countries, were also breaking the norm. Through great effort, ideas began to emerge both in our school and others about what was working. Something was happening. And it was not, thank goodness, the typical middle school experience.

Instead of the classic checked-out middle schooler, we saw students who spoke to adults with humor and authenticity. We saw students leading sophisticated conflict-resolution processes that would challenge many of us adults. We saw them taking on responsibility and using it well, whether they were navigating city streets on their own or camping solo in a forest. And time and again, we saw them complete academic projects with work quality and insights that surprised everyone. When they presented to experts ranging from architects to entrepreneurs to civil rights attorneys, they shared work that was original, well-researched, and from the heart.

And they were still middle schoolers. They were frequently ensnared in social drama. They could be mean at times, though they were usually far harsher on themselves than anyone else. And like some kind of quantum particle, they could be in two states of maturity at almost the same time. I remember watching a group have a class discussion about what it meant to be happy. They were speaking from their own experience and also weaving in ideas from ancient Greece and from Buddhism, so skillfully and with such good listening that my jaw was on the floor. And about thirty seconds after this conversation ended, these very same students were making fart jokes as they jostled each other in the hallway. Right on target. The experience of a great middle school will open them to far more of their potential, but it will not and should not turn them into mini-adults. They're kids but with far more capability than we give them credit for.

I would be the first to say that no one has figured out *the* model for middle school, because there is no one type of school that is right for every student. That said, in the wave of innovative schools that have emerged in recent years, there are themes emerging about how to transform middle schools. In the chapters ahead we'll explore four of these themes: the self-cultivation work undertaken by the adults; a deep advisory program; project-based learning; and an approach to using time more generously in schools.

Across these many experiments there was also a deeper change at play, more important than any one theme. Our sense of what it meant to be an educator was transforming. We were taking off our teacher masks and showing more of ourselves and our emotions. We were rediscovering old interests and passions and letting them shape our classes. We were attempting to be open and honest with each other as an adult team, facing tensions and conflicts, not always masterfully but with determination to learn from them. We were becoming something different from what the word "teacher" conjures up in our culture. Borrowing from the Montessori tradition, several schools decided to call educators something different: guides.

Much like parents receive an invitation to transform at this age, shifting from the boss of a younger child to the companion of an adolescent, we teachers also receive this invitation. Perhaps you were taught in a more traditional way, with a teacher who kept some distance and relayed information through lectures and texts. Perhaps you were trained to be this way. The invitation now, reading this, is to transform your role. To become something like a wilderness guide accompanying your students on a most extraordinary adventure. This is where we'll begin our exploration.

15

BECOMING A GUIDE

When the kids leave the building, schools become strangely empty spaces. It's a quiet but charged time, an invitation to pause. What if we slowed down for a moment? What if we used some of this time to offer our caregiver spirit to ourselves and our fellow educators?

Imagine if, instead of attending meetings or preparing tomorrow's classes, a gathering took place during these quiet after-school hours. A few colleagues prepare a room, creating a circle of chairs, putting snacks on a side table. They're making a space to recharge—an advisory program for adults.

You walk into this space and are greeted by a fellow educator, a rotating moderator for this advisory group of faculty. They offer a moment of mindfulness, a way to center yourself after a day of juggling all your responsibilities. Next comes a simple invitation to check in. *How are you doing?* In the busy environment of a school a question like this can be radical, if asked honestly and accompanied by deep listening.

In this space, colleagues can respond as openly as they wish. Some might speak about work, others more about their personal lives. The group listens, sometimes offering empathy or advice or questions. We employ the same tools we offer students in advisory: ways to ask deeper questions, to show empathy clearly, to offer perspective. The purpose is not to fix anyone. It's to be a group of close colleagues on an adventure together, being honest about what is happening in our lives and growing together with the tools available.

Educators in these groups do this work first for ourselves, because being an educator is hard, and being an adult is hard, and it goes better with support. As a close second, we do it for our students. We know that if we receive the benefit of a close-knit advisory group, and have a felt sense for what it is like to be in one, that will guide us in creating the same space for our students.

Adults who are willing to do this work—the messy process of self-cultivation—are who middle schoolers need. This kind of adult is forever a work in progress, open and curious, willing to share themselves authentically. This makes them seem weird sometimes, meaning honest, and if we're honest we all have weird or quirky elements to ourselves. Middle schoolers can relate to this. They need to see this in the adults around them, to see grown-ups who are self-reflective, growing, trying new things, acknowledging failures, and continuing onward.

This ability to work on yourself with self-awareness and humility is one of the qualifications to become a guide. Borrowing from the Montessori tradition, we chose this term for the educators at Millennium School to signal that we were trying something different. The word "teacher" too quickly brings us to a mental image of someone standing while we are sitting, someone at the front of the room, distant, distributing knowledge. The word "guide," we hoped, meant something else: walking alongside you. Scaling the mountain together. More knowledgeable and experienced, with the natural authority that comes with that, but not holding it over you.

So how does one become a guide?

I believe that all humans innately want to learn and grow, so that self-cultivation is a natural desire. It gets covered up by trauma, by the modeling we receive, and, sometimes in the profession of teaching, by the exhaustion and frustration that can come with the role. When we invite this spirit of self-cultivation and guiding, we are taking on profound work that may lead to changing school structures and changing our lives as educators. Here are some ways to begin:

1. **Adult advisory.** Many teachers are used to professional development being stiff and dry, a dull day in a conference room a few times per year, often in pursuit of a mandate that someone else decided was important. In contrast, the most powerful professional development work I've seen involves small groups of eight to twelve teachers creating an advisory-like experience for themselves, for their professional *and* personal growth. Taking turns facilitating, they create an honest, open space where colleagues can process emotions, share empathy and advice, discuss tips, and, perhaps most important, feel that they are on a shared journey alongside supportive peers. We need this for our own happiness, and we need it to be reliable companions to our students.

   In an ideal world, such groups would gather at least monthly for one to two hours, offering a regular safe space to make sense of life together, just as we do for our students through advisory. We would use the same tools in areas like mindfulness, how to ask open and honest questions, or how to process emotions. Teams become dramatically closer as a result, able to laugh and cry with each other, to appreciate how intense everyone's life can be. And advisors come away with a deep sense for what authentic conversation should feel like, which shapes how they lead advisories.

2. **Hiring.** Who is hired (and occasionally who is fired) is the single most important type of decision that gets made in a school. Each hiring process offers a chance to shape the school's culture. How can you tilt it toward finding guides

rather than traditional instructors? You might include questions about self-cultivation or ask candidates how they take care of themselves. You could ask which tools for personal growth and awareness they've found most helpful. Without requiring them to divulge personal information, you could explore how willing they are to reflect on their life path with humility and insight. You might set the tone by sharing your own life path in this way.

You could involve students more deeply in the hiring process, which often leads to clear signals around fit, particularly with the role of advisor. If it's possible to invest greater time in the process—an investment that will always pay off for a school—you could also find ways to connect that elicit more of someone's real self, like taking a walk together or talking during unstructured time with students and others.

One last but important note: hiring decisions are one of the areas where our unconscious biases leak in, and this can be especially true when we're trying to use our intuition. Watch yourself for preconceived notions of what someone should say or do to show they're self-aware or open-minded. It may be quite different from your own way. A hiring committee with diverse backgrounds and personalities will help protect against this and other forms of bias.

3. **Modeling from the top.** A mentor once told me that there are three essential phrases a leader must learn: "I don't know," "I changed my mind," and "I was wrong." What a relief it was to get this advice—an antidote to the pressure leaders feel to appear always confident and clear-minded. It's an invitation to be more honest. And if that honesty and authenticity is modeled at the top, then it becomes more possible at every level of the school. This type of

leadership enables adults to do the work of self-cultivation, which inevitably involves discovering mistakes, changing your mind, and not knowing things you would really like to know. It's bolstered by school leaders willing to model and speak to the value of authenticity and personal growth, who believe in adolescents while appreciating that middle school is naturally a messy period of time, like a busy construction site. It helps when school principals are in adult advisory groups themselves (whether with others on-site or in groups of fellow principals), opening themselves to growth and honest sharing and listening.

4. **Social-emotional or mindfulness training.** While there is a wide range of quality in these trainings, work that develops adult social-emotional skills, or the ability to calm and center oneself through mindfulness, will be of great benefit to adults and particularly to those guiding adolescents. It can be problematic to mandate this, but a ready invitation, modeling from leadership, easy and free access to training, and a supportive community of peers exploring these topics together will all build momentum.

5. **Increasing degree of faculty choice.** We explored earlier how those at the Authenticity stage often want greater choice as a form of freedom to express their identity and interests. They tend not to appreciate authoritarian management. This is true not just for adolescents at this stage but also for the adults attempting to model it. For teachers to bring more of their creativity and more of their whole self to their work, they need and deserve more choice in their role. This could involve greater discretion in how to use professional development funds or increasing degrees of choice in teaching methods and even curriculum.

For students, much of the magic in middle school is in their peer relationships. They're entering the social world and relish the chance to work and laugh alongside friends, to experience relationships getting closer, and to go through adventures together. So it is for us as educators, who have lived in this social world for longer and yet who often end up isolated because of the traditional role of teacher. When we evolve into guides, we have a chance to enjoy the social connectedness of our workplace in new ways. The practices in this chapter lead to teams that are closer and more supportive. They invite deeper friendships and can reduce the excessive hierarchy that exists in schools. Here too we have a chance to model, showing students adults who are collaborative and close, working on their relationships and helping each other grow.

CHAPTER SUMMARY

* Of the many changes needed to improve middle schools, there is one transformation at the heart: the shift from a traditional teacher role into the role of guide. Rather than a teacher distributing knowledge or controlling experiences, aim for the spirit of a wilderness guide accompanying students on their adventure.

* Part of the power of this change comes from allowing middle schoolers to see deeper into adults. They need to see, and relate to, adults who are quirky, self-aware, authentic, and working on themselves.

* For faculty to function this way, one of the best supports we can offer is an advisory program for adults. Much like what we aspire to offer students in their advisories, this means a safe space for honest conversation, among a consistent group meeting regularly, in which faculty and staff build trust and connection by sharing their lives and learning tools together.

*   A school leader who is open, humble, and self-aware contributes to this culture as well, as does training in social-emotional tools and mindfulness techniques. Offering faculty a greater degree of choice also helps them bring more of their personal passions and unique skills into the classroom.

For Reflection

Have you had a teacher who was this kind of guide, someone who shaped you without trying to control or formally instruct you? Who were they, and what were their personal qualities?

16

ADVISORY AS THE HEART

I will never forget the Wolfpack. When I look back on my adventures as a new school leader, I think of them first. Eight quirky middle schoolers and one quirky principal. They were my advisory.

We had our first meeting in a forest on the first day of their sixth grade year, everyone nervous and curious about this strange new school. Three years later I saw them walk across a mountain stream high in the Sierra Nevada Mountains, my heart swelling with pride and affection, in the informal ceremony they created to mark the end of their middle school journey. Along the way they grew wildly in height, depth, and connectedness. We had awkward moments, frustrated moments, and more adventures and laughs than I can count. They did not always have their best friends in their advisory, but I'm confident that their advisory was a place of safety and belonging that helped them make sense of their middle school years.

The Wolfpack talked through everything from the best sneakers to how to face failure, from dealing with test anxiety to facing a devastating eating disorder, from crushes to our personalities. We went on field trips together. We got mad at each other sometimes. We wrote notes to each other once a year to say what we admired in each person.

When there's space and support for advisory to be like this, it becomes the heart of a middle school.

Of course, this depth of advisory experience is not (yet) a common thing in middle school. Many schools have a time set aside for advisory but don't use it deeply, in part because teachers are not trained or supported to make it as powerful a space as it could be. Most often, advisory ends up as a loosely supervised classroom where students are working on homework or maybe receiving administrative announcements from the teacher. It's not a bad thing, but it's far from what it could be.

Advisory as it *could be* is a different story altogether. In an ideal situation, advisory is a consistent group of eight to twelve students matched with a facilitator (usually a teacher, sometimes an administrator) who stays with them for all three years of middle school. That adult is trained in advisory facilitation skills, which first means that they know how to make the group a safe and accepting place for each student. This is where adolescents begin to belong in middle school, meeting that most essential developmental need.

With that safety established, things begin to get interesting. Advisory becomes the place where students learn social-emotional skills not in an abstract or dry way but by talking about their actual lives, questions, and struggles. One day a student may share the screaming match they had with their sibling, wondering how they can get out of that cycle. Another day someone may describe the ways they struggle with anxiety. At the next session someone may wonder aloud about how to ask someone to go to the dance with them. In each case, a facilitator may help them gather wisdom from the group, reflect on what they're noticing, or perhaps use a social-emotional tool or mindset. In this way students build social-emotional intelligence far more effectively, gaining tools when they are most relevant, applying them personally. They learn to speak authentically in this safe and confidential space, supporting each other to make sense of adolescent life together.

When advisory like this exists, the bonds become remarkably strong. At some schools, advisories meet every day and even go on regular field trips together. At these schools it's no surprise that when students reflect on their adventures in middle school, most of them speak about the relationship with their advisory as a central source of stability and connection. It's what we all need at this age: a trusted group of peers on an adventure together. This is why advisory is the heart of a great middle school.

For this to happen, advisors need a few kinds of support: training in advisory facilitation skills; tools for social-emotional learning; regular time to prep; and access to a community of practice, meaning fellow advisors with whom they can discuss ideas and challenges. Ideally, they also have the chance to be in an adult advisory group, as described earlier. Of course, this is a lot to ask all at once. Luckily, there are many steps, big and small, that can gradually move a school or a classroom toward deeper and more effective advisory practices.

Small Steps

The following steps can be taken if there's no advisory program, or if advisory exists but isn't yet used for deeper social-emotional learning.

* **Start bringing more of yourself.** You begin to make a space safe for honest conversation when you share more of yourself, whether it's a hobby, an emotion you're feeling in the moment, a story of your past, or a photo of your family or yourself as a middle schooler. Your own vulnerability, intentionally chosen, sends a signal that openness is welcome.

* **Journaling.** Self-reflection is a fundamental skill for advisory and for life. A regular class routine around journaling, perhaps with short prompts, can develop this skill.

* **Class agreements.** Whether in advisory or an academic class, you can increase students' feeling of safety and comfort by creating clear class agreements. Begin by asking students what it would take for them to feel psychologically safe in the space, willing to share their honest thoughts. Then you can form agreements as a class based on those requests. These agreements are best treated as a living document, on display, frequently referenced, and occasionally updated. It might include things like "the right to pass," "no judgment," or a confidentiality rule to prevent gossip about a student's personal information.

* **Create a community of practice.** It only takes finding one other teacher to have the beginning of community, and with it all the benefits of feeling less isolated, having access to a brainstorm partner to swap advisory ideas and questions, and more. This does not have to be a teacher at your school.

* **Offer one-time advisories.** If the time for regular advisory meetings doesn't yet exist, you can create a one-time advisory around a specific topic. This might be an issue in the community, stress around an upcoming test, or a moment to reflect and connect at the beginning or end of a semester.

* **Offer advisory as a club.** If your school has times when clubs can meet, during the school day or after, you could offer an Advisory Club or something with a more playful title, like a "Talking About Life Club."

* **Make time for games that connect.** Whether in formal advisories or not, students often love connecting over games. Choose games that encourage students to share more about their lives or to guess things about each other.

* **Make use of transitions.** During transitions at the beginning or end of a class, consider offering a short prompt to

encourage reflection and sharing. For example, a journal prompt on the board when students arrive, which they could respond to and then share with a partner, or an "exit ticket" prompt to reply to as they leave. It can be as simple as asking them to name a favorite game or movie. It's a chance to bring more of students' personal selves into the classroom and to tap into their curiosity about each other.

* **Have a protocol ready to support deeper conversations.** Sometimes a student will share something surprisingly honest and important, whether invited to or not. If you have a framework in mind for how to respond to these moments, you will be better able to support that student and create an opportunity for the class to build trust and skill. For example, in response to a personal share, you could ask the person sharing if they would like responses of empathy, advice, or questions. This gives them the power to guide the conversation, and lets their peers know what kind of response to offer.

* **Build a conflict-resolution practice.** Whether in your classroom or the school as a whole, having a standard conflict-resolution method prepared *before* an issue arises is key to resolving conflicts effectively. It's one of the best social-emotional teaching opportunities you'll get. Tools like Nonviolent Communication or Restorative Justice are particularly powerful. To take this to the next level, consider creating a peer mediator group of students to help others with conflicts.

Bigger Steps

If you have the opportunity for a deeper focus on advisory, with more time and dedicated resources, here are ways to begin creating

an excellent advisory program as the heart of your school. All of
these are supported by the experience of being in an adult advisory,
as explored in the last chapter.

* **Advisory facilitation training.** The skills to lead excellent
  advisories are not mysterious—the only mystery is why
  they aren't more widely taught in teacher preparation
  programs. Luckily there are organizations and institutes
  offering training in these practices, with several listed in
  Appendix 3. Even for teachers with a strong intuitive grasp
  of advisory work, these trainings can build confidence and
  momentum. They also provide a common language to discuss advisory and a way to talk about the school's dedica-
  tion to this work with parents or other partners.

* **Advisory time.** Having a regular time for advisory is essential, especially one protected as much as possible from
  administrative needs or schedule changes. A good goal is
  one period of forty-five to sixty minutes per week, ideally
  at a time that shows its importance to students (i.e., not
  the last period of the day on a Friday). If the school has the
  opportunity for more advisory periods, even daily, it may
  help to designate one of those as a time for deeper conversation, with the others being more flexible in use.

* **Consistent advisory groups.** Building trust in any group is a
  difficult and sensitive process, and particularly so in a group
  of middle schoolers. Anything you can do to help that
  trust form is worth it. One of the simplest ways is through
  consistent groups. Ideally, the same group of students is
  together in advisory for the full year, and even better, they
  "loop" with their advisor over multiple years. Trust deepens
  over this extended time, and the knowledge that this group
  will last for so long encourages students (and advisors) to
  invest in it. Another small but helpful boost comes when

students choose a name for their advisory. Some schools even give each advisory a small physical mascot, which doubles as a talking piece to be passed around during group conversation.

* **Small groups when possible.** One of the largest challenges to meaningful advisories in schools is group size. An ideal advisory consists of eight to twelve students. This is big enough to have a dynamic and diverse group of students, while not so large that it becomes easy to hide or hard to get a word in. Of course, for most schools a "class" this size is difficult to engineer. Some creativity can help here—for example, splitting a class into advisory for one half while the other half goes to the library or to an elective. Or two teachers can combine classes, taking turns so that one teacher can have a half-class advisory while the other takes the overflow students.

* **Shared adventures.** An advisory at its best is a group of young people on an adventure together, experiencing highs and lows and growing closer through both. The more room they have for adventures, the closer they'll become. This could be going on a field trip together or, if there are existing school outings like a wilderness day or a ropes course, using advisory as the grouping for these. With each adventure together, they add to their stockpile of stories and legends—"Remember that time we all got on the wrong bus?!"—which glue the group together.

* **Advisory lead team.** If advisory is being introduced or deepened as a school-wide initiative, it can help to have a small team of lead advisors. This might be one teacher from each grade, for example. Such a team can receive extra training and support, determine themes for advisory conversations, respond to questions of practice from teachers,

and provide a backstop for those who are struggling to settle into the role of advisor.

Whether with small or big steps, walking toward this kind of advisory experience is an essential part of the journey from teacher to guide. As an advisor, you'll have the chance to guide your crew as they go through the natural social and emotional ups and downs of adolescence. You offer the reliability of your warm presence, a safe space to belong and to discuss, and sometimes a tool or perspective to help them through. You'll likely become quite attached to your advisees. Don't be surprised if advising becomes some of the most satisfying work you get to do as an educator.

———————— CHAPTER SUMMARY ————————

* Advisory in a typical middle school is often a casual time to work on homework or receive announcements from a teacher. It's not a bad thing, but it misses a very special opportunity.

* Advisory as it *could be*, when teachers are trained and supported, is something quite different. It becomes a group that offers real safety and acceptance to students, where they can honestly process the ups and downs of adolescence. It's the best place for social-emotional learning, because tools are offered in response to the real questions and struggles that students bring. This kind of advisory is the heart of a great middle school.

* High-quality advisories ideally have small student groups (eight to twelve students is optimal) who meet at least weekly for a year or more, with a consistent advisor. That advisor could be a teacher or administrator and should be supported with training in advisory facilitation skills, social-emotional curriculum, regular time to prep for advisory, and access to a community of practice of other advisors.

* There are big and small steps to take toward this vision of advisory. Small steps include incorporating a journaling practice, offering one-time advisories, creating an advisory club, or teaching a conflict-resolution method. Bigger steps include building in time for a weekly forty-five-to-sixty-minute advisory session, protected from administrative needs, with support and training for the advisors involved.

For Reflection

Have you had the experience of being part of a group where you could be completely honest and which helped you through an intense time of life? What made this group work? If you haven't had this exact experience, what is the closest parallel in your life?

17

LEARNING AS ADVENTURE

At the core of my beliefs as an educator is that learning is innately motivating. Middle schoolers in particular are a motivated bunch. They are intensely curious, intensely engaged in figuring out how their life is evolving. If they appear otherwise, or if we find ourselves resorting to heavy rewards and punishments, then something has gone wrong.

If a student comes to mind as you read this, and you find yourself despairing that they will ever have genuine interest in your academic domain, that is not exactly what I mean. I don't know if, say, social studies will interest them, at least as typically presented. But I do know this: they are highly interested in themselves and how they're growing, they're interested in their peers, and they're interested in figuring out aspects of the real world beyond school and family. Our job is to connect these ready and abundant sources of motivation to the learning we hope for them.

And just how do we do this? By tapping into their developmental drives, described in part 1, as our energy source for a class. We'll examine each of these in turn—the drive for authentic identity, for connection, and for real-world contribution—with an eye toward creating learning experiences that help students complete their developmental tasks. If you do, you'll find that they are engaged and motivated far more of the time, and that they are more likely to actually remember the content learned, because it is infused with emotion and relevance.

Before we go into the specifics, let's try out a new term for this. This kind of learning—emotional, personal, social, tied closely to real-world problems and ideas—is not like the classes that you and I probably attended in middle school. Traditional teaching often makes for machine-like classes, in which we motor along steadily, fifty minutes per day, every day, every week and month. Of course, great teachers rise above this and engage students anyway, but such a learning design makes it harder to be a great teacher.

The kind of learning we're describing here is meant to be an *adventure*. Adventure meaning a group seeking something greater than themselves, connecting through ups and downs, and ultimately making memories that define who they are. Such adventures will have many fun moments, but they also contain struggle and difficulty. In exchange they offer meaning, a sense that participants have lived through something worthwhile and grown as a result. Perhaps it's no surprise that when you ask adolescents about their future hopes, the word "adventure" often finds its way in there.

Adventure is also our metaphor of choice because it speaks to how our brains work. Adventures are emotional, and we know from neuroscience that information with more emotional content is retained better, whereas emotionless information is often forgotten. It is as though our brains, ever careful to prune away unneeded information, conclude that dry, emotionless content must not be that important and so can be deleted. Adventures, on the other hand, show their importance because they contain visceral, memorable events that affect our sense of who we are and how capable we are in the world. These ingredients make for powerful academic experiences. Let's explore how they're made.

What Does a Learning Adventure Look Like?

I walked into a gymnasium full of people, nervous chatter coming from the student section in particular. There were rows of tables holding carefully designed models of tiny homes, and then a long table at which several adults, our special guests for the day, were sitting. This was the culmination for a Quest, as Millennium School terms their project-based classes, and it was one of the more memorable and creative ones I've seen.

Six weeks earlier, students had received a Quest question: Can design make a difference? They had explored this question with a focus on one particular situation where we all wished for ways to make a difference: the homelessness crisis in our city. Every day on their way to school, students walked by homeless people, sometimes entire encampments. We had distributed food and care packages, but our efforts felt insignificant. Many students and faculty struggled with deep questions of what our personal responsibility should be, and what the real systemic issues were.

When a real-world topic carries such charge, existing vividly in students' daily lives, we know it's a natural jumping-off point for a learning experience. In this case, a talented teacher named Lindsay led an interdisciplinary Quest to explore this topic. Students first got a crash course on the history and politics of the homelessness situation. Then Lindsay gave them a challenge: Could you design a tiny home, mass manufacturable, that if produced could increase the housing stock available in our overpriced city? Students had a strict budget of $25,000 per unit and had to account for every penny of cost. They also had to incorporate several scientific learning objectives, for example, measuring the heat transfer and insulation values of their home, building an accurate scale model, and even wiring it with working electrical circuits.

Six weeks from receiving that challenge, and fueled by the daily crisis we saw around us, students were in the gymnasium. An expert panel was present, too, including a homeless rights activist, a city government official, and an architect. Students had poured their hearts into their projects, some working at microscopic levels of detail within their scale model, others getting most excited about the financial and mathematical challenge of making this work within their budget.

Presentation time came, and I could tell the students were nervous. With eyes warily on the expert panel, they walked to the front and began to speak. They shared their understanding of the homelessness crisis, and then how they had designed a low-cost home in response. They were working hard to cram all they had learned into a few minutes' talk. As they spoke, I watched them begin to notice the response. The experts were taking them seriously. They were interested and impressed.

I was standing in the back of the gym beaming at them, knowing that the students had surprised themselves. They had completed a complex project, driven by their own ideas, and presented it to experts whose feedback was both serious and encouraging. This project had pushed them to work with their hands and hearts, to understand both scientific and political issues, to collaborate, and now, to present to adults who grappled with these exact same questions. While a project like this does not immediately solve a public crisis, it *does* create the kind of people who can solve it down the road.

It's a mark of a good Quest that students don't think of it as simply a science or social studies class, though both of those domains were present in this challenge. Students absorbed the academic content because it helped their team solve a problem they cared about. And in the course of struggling with that problem, they made memories that will help define their sense of what they can do in the world. That's what a Quest can do.

With this example in mind, let's consider how to add the spirit of a Quest to a more traditional class.

Step 1: Organize Around a Question

Does "4th-period English Language Arts" sound like an invitation to an adventure? No, it doesn't to me either. And I love writing and reading in the English language. If we're going to go on an adventure, we'll need something other than an academic domain as a title.

An adventure is driven by a *question*. It might be something like "How are we connected?" for an introduction to ecology and life sciences while speaking to a question often on middle schoolers' minds about their social lives. Or "What makes me happy?" for an English and social studies dive into ideas of the good life from novels and different cultures, leading to students writing an essay with their own answer. These are learning adventures, interdisciplinary, real life, a bit mysterious. There is no answer key at the back of the book for these. If the question can be answered by typing it into Google, it's not worthy of an adventure.

Step 2: Ride the Developmental River

The second step is to connect the class experience to the developmental questions we explored in part 1. Remember what motivates middle schoolers most: the drives to discover personal identity (Who am I?), relate to peers (How do I connect?), and feel valuable in the real world (What will I contribute?). To make academics worth their attention, we have to make sure that classes help them answer these questions. This is our job, after all: to create the conditions for adolescents to complete their developmental tasks and find authentic answers to their key questions.

One way to put this into practice is with the concept of a "learning loop." This loop travels through the three developmental questions, going from the personal to the social to the real world, at each stop picking up energy by tapping into developmental drives. Here's an example I stumbled upon one day while popping my head into a class being taught by a magical educator named Simon.

Simon opened the class with a journal prompt, which students had a few minutes to think about: Can you think of a time when you were sure you were right but turned out to be wrong? This was the first stop of the loop, the personal.

After everyone had some beginning ideas, he asked them to share with a neighbor, and then invited a few to share theirs with the class as a whole, prompting several interesting and funny stories. This was the second stop, the social.

Then he introduced the topic they would be exploring that day: the Israeli-Palestinian conflict. Here, he suggested, we're going to learn about people in conflict who are each sure they are right. It might be the most vexing conflict in the world. We're going to simulate various roles together, then use debate to see if we can arrive at some answers. This was the third stop, the connection to the real world. A formidable problem, worthy of adult attention and concern, and thus worthy of students' interest.

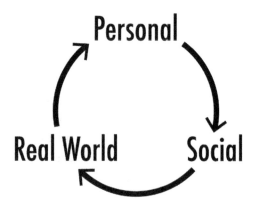

As students began tackling this real-world problem, debating it thoughtfully with peers, they began to see themselves as capable of having a real opinion on important issues. Here is the connection back to the personal, continuing the loop. Meaningful experience with a real problem begins to shift your identity. Students are excited to realize they have something to say about a problem that adults struggle with. Then they want to tell people about it. And the loop goes on. With each stop, new energy is gained, motivation to learn is fueled, and developmental work is being done.

Step 3: The Authentic Audience

If I could point to one single change that has the biggest impact on the quality of student work, it would be the addition of an authentic audience.

To offer a sense of real-world relevance, the audience for students' final work in a given project or semester needs to be *objective* adults. Students know that their teachers and parents are not objective. We know them too well and we're on their side, even when we are trying to push them or hold them to higher expectations. An authentic, objective audience for their work means people whose expertise or lived experience gives them obvious credibility for the topic at hand.

If you're doing a project around Newton's laws and rocketry, your authentic audience might be a panel of engineers. If you're exploring racism and social justice, your authentic audience might include a civil rights attorney, an activist, or someone who has suffered profoundly in their life because of racism. If you're writing children's books about overlooked figures in history, your authentic audience might include authors, a publisher, or an editor. All of these are actual examples of Quests.

When you add an authentic audience, you elevate the project. There is a natural gravitas to the arrival of these special guests. When students know that at the end of their Quest inquiry they'll be presenting to experts, motivation is high, and nerves are present too. So long as these nerves aren't debilitating and are met with useful social-emotional tools to manage them, they can add a useful intensity to a project. These final presentation experiences are faced alongside peers, imbued with emotion, and often lead students to be surprised at how capable they are. All of this makes them an essential and memorable part of a learning adventure.

What's more, when you allow an authentic audience to do some of the assessment, it places teachers and students on the same team. Instead of teachers flipping between being alongside a student as coaches, and then suddenly judging them and handing down a grade, they are now firmly by their side. Teachers may also feel a healthy nervousness leading up to the final presentation, as they want to make sure students present their skills well. They know that the authentic audience has no preexisting relationship to make them subjective.

When the big day comes at the end of each Quest, students discover that they can stand in front of an expert audience and present meaningful work. They see objective adults commenting on it and taking them seriously. Repeat this again and again, project after project, and it becomes part of their identity. This is part of why, at schools like this, middle schoolers look adults in the eye and know they can do things in the world.

Steps Toward Quest Teaching

Consider the following list as a series of steps from traditional teaching toward Quest-style projects, knowing that any worthwhile change will take time and patience:

* **Make it personal.** Warm-up a class with a question or journal prompt inviting self-reflection, ideally forming a bridge to the topic you want to explore that day.

* **Make it social.** Whenever possible, invite students to share their reflections or work with a peer, activating their social motivation.

* **Connect it to the real world.** Find a connection between an upcoming unit and a real-world question, problem, or news headline or to a common challenge affecting tweens and teens.

* **Work in project teams.** Tap middle schoolers' social drive by adding a team element to your class or unit.

* **Lecture less.** Reduce lecture time in class, assigning that material as homework instead, and use more class time for discussion and group work.

* **Mix disciplines.** Integrate elements from another academic discipline, like adding art to a science project. You'll capture more student interest and develop their abilities to flexibly blend academic disciplines and even different ways of thinking about problems.

* **Add an authentic audience.** Even if online-only or asynchronous, and even if the authentic audience is just one person, it's an excellent start. An ideal to build up to would be a panel of experts receiving live presentations from students at the conclusion of a unit or project. Remember that expertise does not just mean academic or work credentials—people with lived experiences lend just as much gravitas to your project.

* **Invite guest speakers.** As a slightly lower-stakes way to include an expert, identify a guest speaker, or lean on parents or friends to find someone, who can offer their thoughts on the topic through a virtual or in-person talk and Q&A with students. Make sure to prepare the guest speaker for an interactive session so that they don't default to a lecture.

* **Break down barriers.** Add a gallery walk or similar structure that allows students to see each other's work, so that projects are not isolated and individual. Middle schoolers

are naturally curious about what others have done, and peer work examples often provide relatable and concrete ways to improve their own.

* **Create a culmination.** In place of or in addition to something turned in to a teacher, create a culmination event in which students' final work is presented to or displayed for others.

* **Invite self-assessment.** Invite students to self-assess their work, based on a clear rubric or other structure, before they see expert or teacher assessments. Then, notice and explore the differences between the student and adult assessments, so that students can become more accurate self-assessors.

With these elements in play, classes become something more than the typical: they become memorable. Perhaps that's the goal that clarifies our task most. How could our classes form positive memories that last for years or even decades? After all, middle school is not a time to "just get through" so you can get to high school—it is one of the richest and most consequential zones of learning in our lives. Let's make the academics reflect that.

--------- CHAPTER SUMMARY ---------

* Middle schoolers are naturally motivated to learn. To create deep academic learning, we have to find links between their existing developmental motivations—which make them curious about identity, relationships, and real-world issues—and our curriculum.

* This deeper learning requires a spirit of *adventure*. An adventure speaks to experiences that are not predefined, where there is no answer key; it makes space for both excitement and struggle; and it promises to create meaning and lasting memories.

✳ Learning as adventure is not just a romantic ideal—it speaks to how our brains retain information. When content is emotionless, studied in isolation, and lacking obvious relevance, we are more likely to forget it. When it's learned in ways that are emotional, social, and connected to real-world issues, it has what neuroscientists call *saliency*, meaning that our brains assign it more importance and thus are more likely to retain it.

✳ A key step to lift the quality of student work is to add an *authentic audience*. This means objective adults, not parents or teachers, who have expertise or life experience in the topic being studied. Their presence lends gravitas to final projects, and puts teachers and students on the same team, wanting to present their best work to these experts.

✳ Even within traditional schools, we can make steps toward this Quest style of teaching. Teachers can add elements that link topics to personal questions, require student collaboration, or involve someone from the "real world" visiting or reviewing work, among many other steps.

For Reflection

What are the most memorable and positive adventures you've experienced? What were the qualities of those adventures? How could those qualities find their way into your work with young people?

18

GENEROSITY WITH TIME

Frederick Taylor lived in an interesting moment in history. Factories were the driving forces of our economy. A spirit of scientific innovation was in the air. A movement was under way to build public schools for every child. The time was the late 1800s, and Taylor had a major role to play. He was the champion of the *industrial efficiency movement*, sometimes called Taylorism, and it aspired to no less than the perfect management of time.

Taylor's approach promised to help factory managers and owners increase the productivity of their employees. Each task was studied and then ascribed an exact number of minutes, enabling worker output to be monitored and maximized. He believed there was a "one best way" to complete each task, so the key was to learn and then enforce that one way, down to the number of seconds each worker should spend. His methods had profound impact in the factories of the day. Some modern-day writers even credit him with inventing the science of productivity.

Why does this matter? At precisely the same time that Taylor was revolutionizing industry, modern public schooling was being introduced in the United States and other western industrialized nations. And what were these brand-new public schools going to base their design on? You guessed it—the exciting, new, scientific-sounding methods that were popular in industry at the time. We would slice learning into small fragments, make sure that each student studied in the "one best way," and then monitor them closely so that everyone was highly productive and proceeded at exactly the same pace.

And so here we are, well over a century after the founding of modern schooling, and these same ideas are still in vogue. Taylor's writing from 1911 sounds like the language of those who pushed for high-stakes standardized testing in the early 2000s: "It is only through enforced standardization of methods, enforced adoption of the best implements and working conditions, and enforced cooperation that this faster work can be assured."

Alas, this approach has landed us in a heap of trouble. Taylor's methods originated on shop floors and particularly in the production of steel, and perhaps there is more validity to his certainty in the "one right way" when molding metal. But when his methods are applied to students in schools, in virtually every way they are ineffective, harmful, and disproven by modern learning science. They make us anxious, distract us from deeper learning, and stigmatize those who learn differently. It's time for a shift. And the place for that shift might just be middle school.

In children's early elementary years, adults often have a relatively relaxed attitude about time. It's easier to see the importance of play, and more obvious that sitting at desks all day is unnatural. It's easier to trust that kids develop differently but that things will get straightened out in the many years of academic learning ahead.

Something happens to this relative ease when children arrive in middle school. Perhaps it's the prospect of high school over the horizon and a fear that a child may be "behind" or have so much to cover to get ready for high school and ultimately be competitive in college applications. Perhaps when parents witness puberty and all the changes it brings, they see their own time and influence with their children diminishing. Likely it is all of those reasons and more, and the result is that we begin to put more and more pressure on middle schoolers' schedules.

Teachers and administrators may receive pressure to track "instructional minutes" per subject. Time for exercise and socializing, or even to eat lunch, is cut back in favor of more seat time in class. Even the schedules in many middle schools betray an anxious attitude toward time, as when a class begins at an odd time like 1:21. This might be a schedule to feed into a machine, but few humans function with that kind of precision. Excessive precision with time is a sure sign that we're not in good relationship to it.

The alternative is a spirit of generosity with time. Instead of a day filled with fragmented blocks of 45 minutes to an hour, consider designing long blocks for students' core projects, up to two to three hours each. Include a break in the middle for movement and social time, and combine a mix of instruction, independent time, and group work. Instead of packing Monday through Friday with the same rotation of academic classes, consider a mid-week change of pace, offering extended time on Wednesdays for Advisory work, or for expeditions to get out of the building and connect with the people, workplaces, and natural spaces around the school. Many schools have found that time taken away from academics for this purpose is more than made up for by increased focus and motivation in the remaining days of the week.

This spirit of generosity ideally begins at the very start of the school day. Instead of heading straight into classes, consider beginning with a morning meeting. For small schools, the entire grade or even school may be able to gather in the same place. I've seen beautiful morning meeting practices in which students enter a common space to music playing, as a nonverbal cue to share in a collective experience. They are then led by rotating student moderators who facilitate the meeting. The student in charge that day may offer a few minutes of mindfulness, and then calls on students or adults with announcements or questions. Both teachers and students get to begin their school day by literally seeing their whole community gathered together, answering questions, and enjoying a peaceful moment.

Further into the day, there are more opportunities to create a healthy relationship with time. A key is to provide ample time for eating and socializing, through both a morning break and a forty-five-minute lunch period. This aligns with the research that longer lunches lead students to eat more healthfully. It also provides time to socialize, hang out in clubs, play a game of pick-up basketball, read a book, or do whatever else they need to recharge..

Recognizing that major schedule changes can be hard to accomplish, there are still many ways to make improvements in more traditional school environments. Here are some suggestions to invite both teachers and students into a more generous relationship with time:

* **Create subunits** to break up semesters into more manageable and motivating lengths of time. Having four quarters, or even five terms per year, creates more regular opportunities to share final work and for students to refresh themselves by taking on a new challenge or problem.

* **Advocate for later school start times,** 8:30 A.M. at the earliest, which support better adolescent mental and physical health as well as greater focus in class.

* **Consider flipping the roles of homework and classwork,** making class more open for discussion and collaborative work while more of the "information transfer" aspects happen at home. This is a generalization and not simple to implement, but even small steps in this direction can open up time for a more exploratory, less time-pressured atmosphere in class.

* **Advocate for block schedules,** or longer stretches (more than the typical forty-five to sixty minutes) of class time.

It's essential, though, that this is done alongside engaging, participatory teaching styles.

* **Be careful not to overfill schedules.** In schools, this may mean allowing more time for socializing, including a less structured homeroom or "flex" period. It may mean offering movement and snack breaks during the day. For parents, this may mean signing your child up for fewer activities and taking leaps of faith about how they might handle more unstructured time. This is not to say that all after-school activities are bad, far from it, but if your child has a packed schedule from breakfast until after dinner or even later, something might be off. It may be worth examining if you hold assumptions about what will happen if they have open time—the classic "idle hands are the devil's workshop" fear—which often is both untrue and unfair to middle schoolers, who need down time and who can be creative and inventive without adult guidance.

These questions of time are not just administrative decisions. In fact, more than most variables, our attitude toward time underlies many of our parenting and teaching choices. *Do I have time to teach them how to do this, or do I need to do it for them? Can I risk them making a long, mistaken detour in their learning? What if they don't finish Algebra 1 by the end of eighth grade? Can I make time for this social-emotional crisis if it will derail my schedule today?*

I believe that our anxious relationship with time is at the heart of many mistakes we make as both parents and teachers. It leads us to a highly controlling mentality, which goes exactly against the development need of middle schoolers to feel more independent, to be tested with more autonomy and choice. It can make students passive, with so little time for their own interests and so much academic busywork that they simply wait for the next instruction or the next activity to start. They may be genuinely unsure how they could manage their own time, if they rarely have the chance to practice.

Our task, then, in whatever role we hold in the middle school world, is to find our own greater ease with time, make peace with it, and then convey that wisdom to the young people in our charge. There is great value in time to socialize or stare out the window. There's value to being lost in time, forgetting to track it while captivated by an activity. Let's stop puncturing these moments with the constant bells of the school day or overfilled activity schedules.

CHAPTER SUMMARY

* When public schools were created in the late 1800s, they were influenced by a popular movement known as *industrial efficiency*. Schools were seen as factories, where every task could be assigned a specific number of minutes, and every student should move at the same pace, as if on a production line.

* This factory approach has been disastrous for learning. In treating young people like identical machines, it creates classes that are boring and impersonal, makes everyone anxious about time, and biases schools against those who learn in different ways.

* Middle school is often when adults shift toward a higher-pressure, time-anxious mentality. This leads us to be highly controlling, which goes directly against the developmental need middle schoolers have to be trusted with more autonomy.

* There are many ways schools can begin breaking out of this mindset: breaking semesters into quarters, particularly combined with project-based work; creating block schedules with interactive classes lasting longer than the usual forty-five to sixty minutes; and making sure that students have enough time to socialize, move, and eat lunch without rushing each day.

* As parents, we can also consider if we have a stressed relationship with time, and how we might be imposing that on our children. If we fear that "idle time" will lead to problems, we may not be giving middle schoolers enough credit. Like us, middle schoolers need open time to wander, be creative, or simply daydream. It will support them in being more active, self-aware learners the rest of the time.

For Reflection

How is your relationship with time? When do you feel anxious about time, and when do you lose track of it? How do you tend to speak about time with the children in your life?

PART 4

FROM RIVER
TO OCEAN

As a middle school leader, I faced a difficult decision one year when one of the teachers I respected most shared his plan for a trip to Washington, DC. At the center of his plan was an afternoon in which the students, about thirty seventh-graders, would be free to wander around Washington on their own. No parents. No chaperones. No teachers. Just a group of thirteen-year-olds wandering the city, in pairs or small groups. Would I approve this trip?

The decision of course was an easy one, as any principal in their right mind would say a firm *no*. The risks are all too easy to imagine. In my mind's eye I saw a lost student wandering cold urban streets, or worse.

But I said yes. The trip went forward. Multiple times. And perhaps it is no surprise to say that, while the students saw many extraordinary things in Washington, what they talked most about was being trusted with independence. This one teacher, a visionary educator if ever I met one, knew that our students yearned for more independence, to be trusted with responsibility. He knew they needed this for their growth. Of course, there was preparation, and meeting spots and phone numbers memorized, but there was risk as well, undeniably. And it was worth it.

It's interesting that the students briefly wandering the streets of Washington were around thirteen years old, as in many traditions and indigenous cultures that is when young people are welcomed into adulthood. It's the age of the Jewish coming-of-age ceremony, the bar mitzvah or bat mitzvah. It's the age when many young people historically were given responsibilities to care for their family, perform crucial community functions, or provide economically.

That doesn't mean we should stop schooling and send kids off to work. It *does* mean that middle schoolers are ready for more responsibility than we think. At the age when people were once coming of age and entering adulthood, today's young people have to ask for permission to use the bathroom and have to hear again and again that they are immature and hormonal. These low expectations cause many early adolescents to feel underappreciated, mistrusted, and misunderstood. The worst result of all might be when middle schoolers begin to believe these low expectations and feel that they can't be trusted with any meaningful responsibility.

That it was a tricky decision, and perhaps a surprising one, to let thirteen-year-olds explore Washington, DC on their own for a single afternoon is a sign of how low our expectations have become. But the fact that the students did so well with this responsibility, and found it such an uplifting and memorable experience, shows how easily we can begin to change this story. It's time to reset our expectations.

19

RESETTING EXPECTATIONS

At a time when I was stuck in fear and anxiety, a dear friend gave me the advice to "make a better story." He didn't mean that I should invent something untrue—he was gently reminding me that I was locked on to the negative parts of my experience and missing the positive. We as a culture do this with middle school, so let's try to apply his medicine in response: What better stories can be found?

We'll explore a handful of better stories, each a tale of what middle school could be and of who middle schoolers really are. I invite you to add them to your collection of stories about this age. Not only do we adults need better stories, but young people deserve to be welcomed into adolescence with optimism and excitement for the magical transformation ahead.

Jiyu Gakuen

At Jiyu Gakuen, a boarding school outside of Tokyo, middle schoolers live in a dormitory completely on their own. There are no adults living with them, and it is no *Lord of the Flies*. In fact, quite the opposite. The middle schoolers manage the building, the food gardens outside, the kitchen and cafeteria, and the budget, down to the penny.

One day at lunch, I sat down with more than 100 students. We were served by one "family" group of eight students who had prepared the lunch. After serving a delicious made-from-scratch meal that included freshly baked bread, the students proceeded to give a detailed presentation on the health data of the meal (total calories, amount of protein, fat, etc.) and then an equally detailed accounting of how they were managing their food budget. I had to smile when they solemnly informed us that their meal, for over 100 people, had come in $1.50 over budget. They had a whiteboard showing the over/under budget figures for each meal they had made, all calculated by students. This was just a normal day in their life but an unforgettable moment in mine, when I saw how I needed to raise my expectations.

ESBZ

At Evangelische Schule Berlin Zentrum (ESBZ) in Berlin, groups of middle schoolers complete a special three-week course whose title translates roughly to "Challenge." In this course, middle schoolers form a group of at least four students and take on a personal quest, with support from one teacher and with a budget of 150 euros each. I spoke with a group who wanted to bike through the German countryside, but because 150 euros would not get them far, they decided they would work each day to earn their room and board each night. The experience of working and cycling through their country was a profound and thrilling adventure. They came away with a sense of how communal their society is, a lesson that could never have been conveyed in a classroom.

Millennium

At Millennium School, and elsewhere where techniques like Nonviolent Communication are taught, middle schoolers can lead conflict resolution processes that would challenge even us adults. Once on a field trip, I saw a small group of students walk away to the edge of a field, talk for a time, and come back. I later learned that before that gathering, a conflict had erupted over some unkind or misinterpreted words, and then a student trained as a peer mediator had stepped in and suggested a conflict-resolution process. The aggrieved parties were asked to reflect on what had happened, separate objective facts from their emotions and assumptions, acknowledge any part they played, and set out their hopes for a repair.

They shared these reflections with each other, using active listening to absorb them and repeat them back in their own words, so the other party felt heard. All of this took place with zero adult involvement. Of course, we had trained them in this method earlier—but at this point, at the average age of twelve, they were capable of managing the process completely on their own. What could have swirled about as rumors and worsening conflict for days was instead over in an hour.

Argonaut

More times than I can count, I have seen middle schoolers create safe conversational space for each other to talk about deep and sensitive issues. In small advisory groups at Argonaut, I've seen students listen with empathy and wisdom to peers who were facing depression, questioning their gender identity, or trying to deal with a complex family situation. I've seen students wisely avoid trying to "fix" someone, instead showing their acceptance and offering advice only when requested. Many of them have a savvy about mental and emotional health that is worlds beyond what I understood as a middle schooler. It makes me hopeful for their generation.

✳

Each example is a signal. Middle schoolers can be both highly independent and *inter*dependent, using their skills to create healthy relationships and team dynamics. Jiyu Gakuen has a beautiful phrase for this with their core value of "autonomous harmony," which I read as the ability to manage oneself while supporting the larger whole—the very opposite of our fearful, *Lord of the Flies* story.

Perhaps these stories can begin to reset our expectations of middle schoolers. We don't need to make them into mini adults, but neither should we treat them like little children or talk about how their hormonal brains can't be trusted. If we raise our expectations, always providing support and patience along the way, they will frequently surprise us and themselves. They are perhaps the most underestimated age group.

Just how do we do this? Recall our discussion of the anchoring effect, which tends to make us—especially parents—underestimate the growing abilities of young people. We need to face our worries, particularly in our pervasively fearful culture of parenthood, and consciously choose to offer adolescents one more degree of risk and responsibility than we are most comfortable with. Our place of ease and comfort is *not* enough for them. If we are not a little uncomfortable, we are probably holding them back.

For parents, look for ways you can offer your child more independence. If you drive them to school, could you drop them off a few blocks away, expanding the radius until they can navigate better and better? Could you give them permission to use public transit, whether going to school or to a friend's house? Teachers, what elements of school could actually be co-facilitated or co-led by students? Could they organize a school event? Vote to choose a project focus? Do part of their grading using self-assessments, based on rubrics you create?

And, of course, these steps are just the beginning. Could students be trusted to arrange their own field trip or even multiday trip? Could they learn to handle themselves in wilderness situations, eventually without active adult help? Could you teach them conflict resolution and trust them, or a select group most interested in the topic, to mediate peers' conflicts? With the right conditions, all of these can be answered affirmatively.

Risk and Time

I have two final suggestions on this path of changing our expectations. The first is that risk cannot be faked. If a situation is artificial—like doing conflict resolution with a scenario on a slip of paper—adolescents will rarely rise to the challenge. They are just too smart to be fooled into caring about it. It's up to us to define a level of acceptable exposure to real-world complexity and risk, and "zero" is not the answer.

In a real-life conflict resolution, there is a risk that the peer mediator will make the wrong move and could even worsen things. In a wilderness situation, a student could be hurt or cold all night if they don't set up their tent properly. On a field trip in a city, a group could get lost. These elements of risk are an essential ingredient to elicit middle schoolers' full motivation, which in turn creates deep learning.

This does not mean we accept all risks or just let them learn the hard way. It means we have to prepare adolescents well. Situations with real risk push us, the parents and educators, to get serious about teaching real-world skills of independence and interdependence. When we know they will soon be tested, students are more motivated to learn, and we are more motivated to teach them well.

The second suggestion is to watch out for anxiety around time. After fear, time anxiety is the bogeyman that most causes us to get in the way of middle schoolers' development. For example, we might want them to learn to make dinner for the family, but we don't have time for their slower and more error-prone process of making a meal. Or we want them to navigate the city streets to school, but we can't spare the time to stand by while they try that out in the midst of a busy morning in our hectic lives. Or in class, we can't let students vote on projects today or take their own unique paths to a final exhibition, because we're behind in our curriculum sequence and we need to catch up.

Some of this is just life—but listen to how often you use the excuse of time to not give them more chances to try and to mess up. Remind yourself that it takes them more time to do something for themselves than for you to do it for them, because they're learning it. But without those opportunities to try, mess up, and tinker toward greater independence and interdependence, they will never develop those skills.

If we make these leaps of faith and lift our expectations, middle school can be an adventure in which students discover who they are and how much they can do in the big social world that is opening to them. Middle school is the turning toward adulthood, after all. If we help open the doors for more freedom and responsibility, with careful preparation, then we'll keep seeing their enthusiasm, and we'll keep being surprised by how capable they are.

CHAPTER SUMMARY

* Our expectations of middle schoolers are often remarkably low, despite the fact that in many cultures this is the time of traditional coming of age ceremonies, when great responsibility is acquired. We systematically underestimate them. Being underestimated leads them to feel that adults are condescending, confused, and more likely an obstacle than a facilitator.

* There are countless examples that light the path toward higher expectations. From managing their own dormitory to handling peer mediation, middle schoolers can do more than we might think.

* When we adults are preoccupied by fears or anxiety about time, we are likely holding young people back. Without overcorrecting, we can take steps to prepare students for more real-world exposure and allow them time for the messy process of building new skills of independence and interdependence.

* Opportunities for these steps are everywhere, from cooking dinner, to getting to school on their own, to leading more of their learning within the school day.

For Reflection

When you were an adolescent, was there an adult who took you more seriously or who thoughtfully gave you more freedom or responsibility? How did you respond, and how do you think the experience affected you?

_____

WHERE THEY GO

We have explored far and wide, and now we come back to where we started. Back to the raft as it surges through whitewater rapids. Back to our core metaphor for adolescence, the river journey propelled by strong development currents. Let's see where we've traveled.

We explored the three strongest currents in this river: a drive toward authentic identity, another toward connection, and a third toward discovering how to contribute in the real world. Perhaps you can see now that every single behavior we witness and every phrase we hear from a middle schooler can be tied back to these core drives. They are never less than earnest explorers of this river.

If middle schoolers appear checked out, they are likely feeling blocked and unable to follow these strong currents. To position ourselves well, we can ask: How are we helping them find answers to their fundamental questions? Are we trying to give them the answer, or are we facilitating experiences in which they'll discover their own answers?

Next we explored the three turns of the river they pass through, each representing a developmental stage available to early adolescents. It begins with Belonging, with the deep need to feel accepted and part of a group, even to the point of welcoming conformity.

When at some point that conformity feels limiting, or as they become more sophisticated observers and players of the games of life, they'll move on to Achievement. Here they see more of the games others play—perhaps for grades, popularity, or athletic glory—and they want to learn the rules and win. To win means to earn respect, or status, in the eyes of others.

At some point, perhaps in later middle school, they may wonder why they are playing these games for others or whether something like a letter grade is really that meaningful. Here they are entering the Authenticity phase, in which they choose which games they want to play, whether they're cool or not. They are integrating the skills and confidence to belong and achieve, and now they want to apply those skills toward something that feels personally meaningful. They're discovering passions and tapping into their full motivation.

Through these stages we see our own roles in a new light. Without doing the work for them, we can create conditions that help them experience these key developmental tasks—finding belonging, finding a source of achievement, and, ultimately, finding their authenticity again—in this social world that their brains can now perceive so intensely. Our new role, whether we are parents or teachers, is akin to that of a wilderness guide, or a companion, and it represents a transformation of the earlier roles of boss or instructor. Now we are walking alongside them, witnessing them, intervening less, putting more energy toward our own aliveness and the mindsets we model for them.

To understand middle schoolers deeply, and thus be of greatest service, we explored the physical practices that support healthy development. To be good companions, it serves to know some of the traps on this road, like the pervasive sleep deprivation among adolescents or the importance of including sensory processing differences when we try to make sense of their behavior. We can appreciate that their behavior is often less top-down or willful than we think, and instead is often body-up, driven by how well they feel within, what they're sensing, and when and how they feel threatened.

We delved into the world of social and emotional intelligence, because this is the epicenter of middle schoolers' learning and growth. Their brains are coming alive to the intense and complex social world around them, and it shakes up every part of their identity. We learned that social-emotional intelligence is a set of teachable skills, not traits they simply are born with or without, and we explored how to offer this essential learning, knowing it will likely have a greater impact on their success as adults than any academic learning.

This naturally took us into middle schools themselves, from efforts to reimagine them from the ground up, to ways we can improve an existing school. We learned what it means to shift from "teacher" to "guide." We saw how advisory, when done well, becomes the heart of a great middle school. And how project-based learning, by tapping into middle schoolers' social drive through teamwork and by pointing them toward real problems and bringing them into contact with real-world adults, can lead to remarkably deep and memorable academic experiences. We even examined our relationship to time, how we've come to always feel rushed and how we might step out of that mindset to allow deeper learning to take place.

But schools can't do it all, even the best ones. So much of middle schoolers' best learning takes place outside of school, yet often we leave this piece to chance, giving it less strategic thought than we would any single academic subject. We explored the wide range of essential experiences, from apprenticeships to rites of passage, that a wise companion can help to make happen for the middle schooler in their life. What if they graduated from middle school having started a business, resolved peer conflicts, or learned to camp on their own under the stars?

Finally, we came to a question: What should we expect of middle schoolers? Knowing what we know now, is it possible that we've underestimated them? The answer is a resounding "yes," because this may be the most underestimated age. With the right support and our confident expectation, they can reach remarkable levels of independence and interdependence during these years.

We have one last turn on this river of development before our metaphor is complete, and this book as well. Where is this river ultimately going?

If all goes well, we'll witness this river open into a vast ocean. This ocean is the wider world of society, the one that our kids and students will blast into, likely well before they seem ready to us. We can only accompany them so far. At some point, we lose them to the ocean.

Or so it seems. If we have accompanied them well, with the experiences and the space they need to develop fully, then they will be capable and bold navigators of the ocean. And if they can do this, then they will be back. They will return to shore to greet you, bringing the gift of their adult selves and insights. It will be a wonder and delight to see them.

Their return to our shore is not a result of how much we obsessed over their academic progress. It's about whether we created the conditions for them to develop as whole humans. It's about whether we evolved with them, becoming companions rather than holding onto the old role of boss.

Let the young person in your life lead the way. This is their quest. They may take it in directions you could not have imagined—in fact, it's best if they do. Your mind's plans would be too small for them.

Leading the way means that they are exercising ever greater independence and interdependence. You are opening the doors, perhaps a touch more quickly than you might like, to the wider world. You're helping to create experiences where they learn what it is to belong, to achieve, and to bring their authentic self into the world. You're holding the knowledge that middle school, far from its sad reputation, is in fact full of magic, a launch into this path of adventure.

Remember the invitation here, the secret gift to you as companion: this is your chance to grow like you haven't since you first became a parent, or perhaps since you were an adolescent yourself. In fact, the more you can dust off those years, working through the layers to find the middle schooler who is still alive within you, the better. Remember your own adolescence—especially the messy parts. Find journals. Talk with friends from that era. Remember your struggles. Keep that emotional current alive. Your struggles may not be the same as your child's or student's, but the intensity likely will be.

As you find that adolescent fervor, apply some of it to your life now. This is your invitation to fan the flames of your own authenticity, your passions and interests in the world, in service to yourself and to the adolescents who need to see alive, engaged, passionate adults around them. Make sure you do this work of growth alongside others, in groups you might find or create of fellow parents and educators. Just as adolescents discover their identities in a social process, we adults need trusted friends as our identities evolve and our growth makes new leaps.

It will not be easy or simple. But it will be an adventure—with all that means, all the ups and downs, and all the magic of personal transformation. I wish you an adventure of profound beauty, surprise, and many joyous reunions on the shore.

ACKNOWLEDGMENTS

I've had the good fortune to come across magical people in life. Little bits of their magic must have rubbed off, and like magnets, these bits point me toward other magical people, ideas, and experiences. A deep bow of gratitude to the following magicians:

Stephen Lessard, a magical teacher if ever there was one, always ready to leap into the river at a moment's notice.

Michael Mervosh, a wizard in everyday attire, whose Hero's Journey Foundation program launched me into another way of being in the world.

My extraordinary editor, Ann Spradlin, whom I first got to know as the caring parent of a wonderful middle schooler, and then later realized was the perfect collaborator for this project.

The generous reviewers who received half-baked prose and helped keep it cooking: Blake Boles, Abigail Henderson, Cheryl Law, Masharika Maddison, Kim Mishkin, Rachel Skerritt, Kim Smith, and Michael Stack.

For Kina Grannis, Emi Grannis, and Jesse Epstein, who show me what a maker's life can be and talked me through the big and little details of the creative process.

For Emi Takemura, whose encouragement gave me confidence that these ideas could be of use to many others.

For Stephanie Kinkel, an exceptional guide to young people, whose beautiful artwork opens each section of the book.

For the remarkable humans of Millennium School, including faculty, staff, parents, and especially students, who trusted me and taught me so much.

For Andrew Ravin and the Workshop Middle School in Brooklyn, New York, who have inspired me and supported this project since the beginning.

For the incredible group of friends and strangers who came together on Kickstarter to support this book's launch, with special thanks to Jo Balme, Gordon & Patricia Grannis, Tomoko Kusamoto, Ari David Paul and Vivek Shah & Pooja Mehta Shah.

And most importantly of all, for the amazing Misa Grannis, my wife and partner, who created the cover design for this book and whose kindness, patience, and love shine through every page.

There are many others I would like to thank, those who have helped this book and the preceding work at Spark, Millennium School, and Argonaut, and those who simply are willing to walk alongside me on the curious paths of life. Thank you!

APPENDIX 1:
Developmental Research

The research and theoretical base for the developmental stages of adolescence is a fascinating topic and makes up many a book in its own right. I have compiled a set of *developmental stage theories* and simplified them into the three stages used in this book (Belonging, Achievement, and Authenticity).

It is important to keep in mind that while intriguing and very useful, stage theories are generalizations. They are not nearly nuanced enough to accurately describe a whole human being. Please don't mistake the map for the actual territory, as the saying goes. Someone's stage is not written in stone—it's simply the place they're most likely to be found right now.

More specifically, this means that in any one day, a person may exhibit a range of stages based on the context. You might act like the Belonging stage around a new team you joined, the Authentic stage with an old friend, and the Achievement stage everywhere else, including work, home, and with other friend groups. There tends to be a "center of gravity" in one stage, the one that comes up the most frequently at a given period in your life. In the example above, that would be the Achievement stage, and it means that's where most of your key developmental tasks are.

Successive stages offer you the capacity to handle more complexity, but they absolutely do not make you a better person. Consider the clear developmental stages of early childhood. If one toddler starts walking at ten months and another at fourteen months, that does not make the early walker a better toddler or a better human. Stage theories should not be used to judge people—their greatest use is in understanding someone better, so that you can be of service.

How might they guide us to help? First, they help us locate what someone is working on. If we pick up signs that a child is at the Belonging stage, then we know that they deeply need to feel accepted by a friend or small group and to begin to explore their identity through that context. We can't do the work for them, but we can interpret their behavior more accurately (and perhaps take things less personally, if our other goals for them don't seem to matter as much to them).

After locating someone, our next task is to help create *stability* within that stage. In the example above of working on the Belonging stage, that may mean helping them find a close friend or group, and then being relatively hands-off while they enjoy and discover what can be learned. Even if they go through a period of conformity, as long as no one is being harmed, we can accept this as a natural part of this stage. They're doing their work, internalizing a deep sense that they can be accepted by and connected to peers.

Once a child has stabilized in a given stage and is completing the developmental tasks at hand, gaining confidence from them, then our job shifts. That child who has been glued to her best friend for all of sixth grade might be ready for more. We no longer need to worry about supporting her to experience Belonging. Now we could challenge her, lovingly and gently, into the next stage. This spirit of *loving challenge* is the next step in supporting someone developmentally.

In this case, a loving challenge might mean creating an invitation to join a second group, one whose values are slightly different. This can help a middle schooler go beyond the Belonging stage, moving toward the realization that they can belong in multiple groups and find a way to achieve respect in each. This is one doorway into the Achievement stage.

We can't rush these things. If someone has not yet settled well into Belonging, it would be unwise to challenge or push them into Achievement. They're already getting invitations from the signals of those around them, both peers and adults, who are at that stage. But they need to first build their foundation in Belonging before they can go on.

So, where do all these stages come from? Below is a partial list of the scientists, psychologists, and philosophers who have created these developmental stage theories. I encountered these theories in my search for a deeper foundation for school design, something that would point us toward realizing human potential rather than simply preparing for the next stage of education.

These thinkers have helped to illuminate what human potential looks like as we develop. No one has a perfect map, but by combining these many viewpoints, we can find patterns and commonalities that point us toward deeper teaching and parenting.

* **Michael Commons** studies complexity science at Harvard. In the 1980s, he developed the model of hierarchical complexity to describe how complex a given behavior is. This led him and colleagues to define sixteen stages of complexity, beginning with levels as basic as what a single-celled organism can do, through concrete and abstract stages, and into levels of metacognition and advanced systems thinking. His stages of concrete, abstract, formal, and systematic align with the developmental stages explored in this book.

* **Susanne Cook-Greuter** is an independent scholar and consultant whose theory of ego development describes several stages of growth. Her stages of conformist, self-conscious, and conscientious correspond roughly to Belonging and Achievement, and her stage called individualist overlaps with Authentic.

✳ **Robert Kegan** is a developmental psychologist and pro-
lific author who proposed "orders of consciousness" to
describe human development based on his research.
Roughly speaking, orders 2 through 4, which speak to the
beginning of logical thinking through the development of
abstract, systems thinking, relate to the stages described in
this book.

✳ **Lawrence Kohlberg** created a well-known extension of
Piaget's theories, which he called the stages of moral
development. His stages 3–5 correspond roughly to those
described in this book, as he charted a growth path from
conforming to social standards, toward awareness of and
respect for different perspectives. This notion of becoming
able to hold multiple perspectives is found in many, if not
all, of the developmental theories presented here.

✳ **Abraham Maslow's** pyramid or "hierarchy of needs" is perhaps the most famous stage theory in popular knowledge.
Maslow proposed that after our basic survival and safety
needs are met, we aim for belonging, then esteem (often
through achievement), and finally self-actualization, in
which we develop and express more of our innate human
potential.

✳ **Jean Piaget** is a legendary developmentalist, one of the
most cited and influential psychologists of the twentieth
century. In Piaget's thinking, the late elementary to early
middle school years were the phase of "concrete operations,"
gradually shifting to "formal operations" from middle to
early high school, in which more abstract thinking and
metacognition become possible.

✳ **Jenny Wade** is a development psychologist and professor
whose holonomic theory aims to describe the evolution of
human consciousness across a lifespan. Four of the stages

she describes, from conformist to authentic consciousness, align with the stages in this book. She is an advisor
and board member at Millennium School, and her book
Changes of Mind is a particular inspiration.

* **Ken Wilber** is a philosopher and the developer of integral
theory, which attempts to create a unified theory of human
development. He describes a range of stages, of which those
from concrete to what he terms "vision-logic" speak to
the drives for Belonging, Achievement, and Authenticity
explored here.

You may be wondering if there are more stages of growth
beyond Authenticity. The short answer is yes. The longer answer
is that many theorists and researchers diverge on what constitutes
these later stages, perhaps because they are so rarely reached. For
many of us, living in a place of authenticity while continuing to
find belonging and achievement in our complex world, is more than
enough challenge. Descriptions of later stages often are defined
more by spiritual realizations, depending on the faith or tradition
being referenced.

In my view, the Buddhist monk and teacher Thich Nhat Hanh
described it most compellingly when he wrote of the stage of *Interbeing*. This stage may resolve some of the dark sides of Authenticity
(alas, every stage has a dark side), which involve excessive individ-
ualism and fatigue from trying so hard to bring your full passions
into our complicated world. In the stage of Interbeing, perhaps, we
put our individual lives in better perspective, with deeper appreciation for the world being both always deeply broken and always
quite perfect, and ourselves as well. We might recognize that, as
Thich Nhat Hanh put it, we "inter-are"—we don't really exist as
individuals without others. We are always in a social mesh, even
if it's one we only carry internally. And here perhaps we have the
road back to middle school, because in these magical years, that

social mesh is revealed. It's a shock for many young people, as their brains develop to allow them to see this fine social web all around them, but it welcomes them onto a path of remarkable growth and transformation.

APPENDIX 2:
How to Create Apprenticeships

In Chapter 14, we explored apprenticeships as one of the most powerful beyond-school learning experiences to offer a middle schooler. My experience with this work comes from having co-founded and led Spark, a nonprofit organization that has created apprenticeships for thousands of middle schoolers around the United States. You can learn more at www.sparkprogram.org.

Here are some pointers to create this kind of experience for the middle schoolers in your life:

* **Readiness check.** Not all middle schoolers are ready for an apprenticeship; it may be worth waiting until seventh or eighth grade for them to get the most out of the experience. Some markers of readiness are: (1) they can usually, not always, manage their time well and remember the most important follow-ups from a conversation: (2) they have the skills and awareness to handle themselves in a professional environment, understanding appropriate boundaries, questions, and communication; and (3) they've demonstrated the ability to commit to an activity for at least a month.

* **Visioning.** Some adolescents will have an instant, strongly felt answer when asked what they want to do—"I want to be a chef!" Others may have a harder time with this question. It helps to remind them that this is *not* a request to decide what they want to do with their lives. The purpose

of this is learning, fun, and exploration. You may also notice that some adolescents have a limited set of options in mind, perhaps only considering the more common professions. Think about ways to expose them to other possibilities, whether through friends with unusual professions, YouTube channels, or shows like the PBS series *Roadtrip Nation*, in which two recent college grads drive around the country interviewing people in a range of careers. When a young person has seen a wide range of choices and can settle on a set of options—ideally two or three—and not change their mind for a few weeks, then you're ready to proceed.

* **Networking.** Now it gets real. As their companion, you have the opportunity to teach one of the most useful yet rarely taught skills: how to put your network to work. You might begin by helping them craft a simple, clear template for an email request, and then by identifying a handful of allies, the peers or adults closest to the young person in question and most likely to be willing to help. They can begin by asking these allies for advice and help, seeing if they can in turn spread the word to their networks. With time and effort, something will emerge, and the process may be among the most useful learning experiences of this journey.

* **Keep asking.** If a series of "no's" come in, it is easy to lose faith. Here we have the chance to foster resilience as you encourage the apprentice seeker to continue asking, to identify new allies, to remind in gentle ways, to hone their message, and to wow potential allies with their politeness and ability to explain why they want this learning experience. It will happen eventually: a young person on an earnest mission to learn can't be refused forever.

* **Clear structure.** Once someone has agreed to offer an apprenticeship, the key is to make sure that the structure is clear. In collaboration with both the middle schooler and the mentor, you can make sure they define a specific schedule and project to frame the experience. This could be the design of a home if the apprenticeship is with an architect; or making a website with a software designer; or a slide presentation on a relevant law with an advocacy organization. Finally, it helps to schedule some kind of final presentation or celebration at the end of the apprenticeship. This could be presenting at a meeting of other employees in the business. Imagine the confidence an adolescent would feel after presenting to a group of experts in a professional setting.

APPENDIX 3:
Advisory Trainings

In chapter 16, we explored why high-quality advisory programs are the heart of a great middle school. The following is a list of organizations which train educators to become excellent advisors. This is far from a comprehensive survey of the field, but will hopefully serve as a beginning point:

Argonaut: www.argonaut.school/for-teachers

The Compass Model from Valor Collegiate Academies: https://poweredbycompass.org/

Expeditionary Learning Crew program: www.eleducation.org

The Institute for Social and Emotional Learning: https://www.instituteforsel.net/

Leaders & Learners Consulting,: http://www.packnetwork.com/leadersandlearners.org/Home.html

Millennium School's Forum method: https://www.millenniumforum.org

Origins Program: www.originsonline.org

PassageWorks Institute: www.passageworks.org

Responsive Classroom: www.responsiveclassroom.org

NOTES

Introduction

page xi *middle school is when academic engagement plunges:* Li, Y., & Lerner, R. M. (2011). Trajectories of school engagement during adolescence: Implications for grades, depression, delinquency, and substance use. *Developmental Psychology, 47*(1), 233–247. https://doi.org/10.1037 /a0021307. *And* Wigfield, A., & Eccles, J. S. (2002). Students' motivation during the middle school years. In J. Aronson (Ed.), *Improving academic achievement: Impact of psychological factors on education* (pp. 159–184). Academic Press.

page xi *conflict at home increases:* De Goede, I. H. A., Branje, S. J. T. & Meeus, W. H. J. (2009). Developmental changes in adolescents' perceptions of relationships with their parents. *Journal of Youth and Adolescence, 38*, 75–88. https://doi.org/10.1007/s10964-008-9286-7

page xi *mental health problems emerge:* Kessler R. C., Berglund P., Demler O., Jin R., Merikangas K. R., & Walters E. E. (2005, June). Lifetime prevalence and age-of-onset distributions of *DSM*-IV disorders in the National Comorbidity Survey Replication. *Archives of General Psychiatry, 62*(6), 593–602. https://doi.org/10.1001/archpsyc.62.6.593

page xi *and bullying, exclusion, and other forms of social harm are inflicted:* Milsom, A., & Gallo, L. L. (2006). Bullying in middle schools: Prevention and intervention. *Middle School Journal, 37*(3), 12–19. https://doi .org/10.1080/00940771.2006.11461531

page xi *the human brain goes through two periods of particularly rapid development:* Dahl, R., Allen, N., Wilbrecht, L. et al. (2018). Importance of investing in adolescence from a developmental science perspective. *Nature*, *554*, 441–450. https://doi.org/10.1038/nature25770. *And* Dahl, R., & Suleiman, A. (2017). Adolescent brain development: Windows of opportunity. In N. Balvin and P. Banati (Eds.), *The adolescent brain: A second window of opportunity—A compendium* (pp. 21–29). UNICEF.

page xi *roughly the middle school years:* There are varying definitions of early adolescence in use among researchers, in part because the beginning of puberty varies significantly across individuals. Some define early adolescence as covering ages 9 to 14, others 10 to 13, and still others 10 to 15. While there is no simple way to integrate these different views, middle school and early adolescence are, at a minimum, highly overlapping.

page xv *Student ratings of school climate and connectedness to teachers:* Wang, M. T., & Dishion, T. J. (2012). The trajectories of adolescents' perceptions of school climate, deviant peer affiliation, and behavioral problems during the middle school years. *Journal of Research on Adolescence*, *22*(1), 40–53. https://doi.org/10.1111/j.1532-7795.2011.00763.x. *And* Way, N., Reddy, R., & Rhodes, J. (2007, Dec.). Students' perceptions of school climate during the middle school years: Associations with trajectories of psychological and behavioral adjustment. *American Journal of Community Psychology*, *40*(3–4), 194–213. https://doi.org/10.1007/s10464-007-9143-y. PMID: 17968655.

page xv *Between 2007 and 2017, the number of US teens reporting depression:* Geiger, A. W., & Davis, L. (2019, July). A growing number of American teenagers—particularly girls—are facing depression. Pew Research Center. https://www.pewresearch.org/fact-tank/2019/07/12/a-growing-number-of-american-teenagers-particularly-girls-are-facing-depression/

page xv *National Institutes of Health report that nearly 1 in 3 US teens:* National Institute of Mental Health. (n.d.). *Any anxiety disorder.* National Institutes of Health. https://www.nimh.nih.gov/health/statistics/any-anxiety-disorder#part_2578, referencing Merikangas, K. R. et al. (2010, Oct.). Lifetime prevalence of mental disorders in US adolescents: Results from the *National Comorbidity Survey Replication—Adolescent Supplement. Journal of the American Academy of Child & Adolescent Psychiatry*, *49*(10), 980–989. PMID: 20855043.

Chapter 1

page 5 *As a medical student she was even:* Kramer, R. (1976). *Maria Montessori.* University of Chicago Press.

page 6 *"This is the time when the social individual is created.":* Montessori, M. (1939). *The "Erdkinder" and the functions of the university.* Maria Montessori Training Organisation. Retrieved from www.montessori.org.

page 6 *brain changes make young people highly sensitized to the social world:* Somerville, L. H. (2013). The teenage brain: Sensitivity to social evaluation. *Current Directions in Psychological Science, 22*(2), 121–127. https://doi.org/10.1177/0963721413476512

page 6 *They become better at reading faces:* Steinberg, L. (2014). Age of opportunity: Lessons from the new science of adolescence (p. 95). Houghton Mifflin Harcourt.

page 6 *They show stronger reactions to expressions of emotion in others:* Burnett, S., Sebastian, C., Cohen Kadosh, K., & Blakemore, S. J. (2011). The social brain in adolescence: Evidence from functional magnetic resonance imaging and behavioural studies. *Neuroscience & Biobehavioral Reviews, 35,* 1654–1664.

page 6 *They become keenly interested in groupings:* Somerville, L. H. (2013). The teenage brain: Sensitivity to social evaluation. *Current Directions in Psychological Science, 22*(2),121–127. https://doi.org/10.1177/0963721413476512

page 7 *It's the perfect neurobiological storm:* Steinberg, L. (2014). Age of opportunity: Lessons from the new science of adolescence (p. 95). Houghton Mifflin Harcourt.

page 7 *emotional volatility peaks during the middle school years:* Larson, R. W., Moneta, G., Richards, M. H., & Wilson, S. (2002, July–Aug.). Continuity, stability, and change in daily emotional experience across adolescence. *Child Development, 73*(4), 1151–1165. https://doi.org/10.1111/1467-8624.00464. PMID: 12146740.

page 9 *Psychologist Mona Delahooke put it well:* Delahooke, M. (2019). Beyond behaviors: Using brain science and compassion to understand and solve children's behavioral challenges (p. 111). PESI Publishing & Media.

page 12 *lifelong musical tastes are often formed at this age:* Jansari, A., &
Parkin, A. J. (1996). Things that go bump in your life: Explaining
the reminiscence bump in autobiographical memory. *Psychology and
Aging, 11*(1), 85–91. *And* Stephens-Davidowitz, S. (2018, February 10).
The songs that bind. *New York Times.*

page 12 *strong emotions help to encode experiences:* Stenson, A. F., Leventon,
J. S., & Bauer, P. J. (2019). Emotion effects on memory from childhood
through adulthood: Consistent enhancement and adult gender differences. *Journal of Experimental Child Psychology, 178*, 121–136.

Chapter 2

page 17 *Steinberg and his colleagues coined a term for this phenomenon: the
"peer effect.":* Steinberg, L. (2014). Age of opportunity: Lessons from the
new science of adolescence (p. 95). Houghton Mifflin Harcourt

Chapter 3

page 26 *middle schoolers should live on and operate a farm and inn:* Montessori, M. (1939). *The "Erdkinder" and the functions of the university.* Maria
Montessori Training Organisation. Retrieved from www.montessori.org.

page 27 *powerful and well-documented bias in human perception:* Furnham,
A., & Boo, H. C. (2011). A literature review of the anchoring effect.
Journal of Socio-Economics, 40(1), 35–42. https://doi.org/10.1016/j.socec
.2010.10.008. ISSN 1053-5357.

Chapter 4

page 34 *The Swiss psychologist Jean Piaget:* Piaget, J. (1971). The theory of
stages in cognitive development. In D. R. Green, M. P. Ford, & G. B.
Flamer (Eds.), *Measurement and Piaget.* McGraw-Hill.

page 34 *Abraham Maslow theorized:* Maslow, A. H. (1943). A theory of
human motivation. *Psychological Review, 50*(4), 370–396. https://doi.org
/10.1037/h0054346

page 34 *Jenny Wade's holonomic theory:* Wade, J. (1996). Changes of mind: A
holonomic theory of the evolution of consciousness. State University of
New York.

page 34 *Michael Commons's model of hierarchical complexity:* Commons, M. L. (2007). Introduction to the model of hierarchical complexity. *Behavioral Development Bulletin, 13*(1), 1–6. https://doi.org/10.1037 /h0100493. ISSN 1942-0722.

Chapter 5

page 41 *feeling they belong is an urgent need:* Tomova, L., Andrews, J. L., & Blakemore, S.-J. (2021). The importance of belonging and the avoidance of social risk taking in adolescence. *Developmental Review, 61,* 100981. https://doi.org/10.1016/j.dr.2021.100981. *And* Korpershoek, H., Canrinus, E. T., Fokkens-Bruinsma, M., & de Boer, H. (2020). The relationships between school belonging and students' motivational, social-emotional, behavioural, and academic outcomes in secondary education: A meta-analytic review. *Research Papers in Education, 35*(6), 641–680. https://doi.org/10.1080/02671522.2019 .1615116

page 42 *students' sense of belonging falls during middle school, as does the related sense of connectedness to school:* Way, N., Reddy, R., & Rhodes, J. (2007, Dec.). Students' perceptions of school climate during the middle school years: Associations with trajectories of psychological and behavioral adjustment. *American Journal of Community Psychology, 40*(3–4), 194–213. https://doi.org/10.1007/s10464-007-9143-y. PMID: 17968655. *And* Wang, M. T., & Dishion, T. J. (2012). The trajectories of adolescents' perceptions of school climate, deviant peer affiliation, and behavioral problems during the middle school years. *Journal of Research on Adolescence, 22*(1), 40–53. https://doi.org /10.1111/j.1532-7795.2011.00763.x

page 44 *Beverly Daniel Tatum described:* Tatum, B. D. (2017). Why are all the Black kids sitting together in the cafeteria? (p. 62). Basic Books.

Chapter 6

page 57 *The concept of the growth mindset:* Dweck, C. S. (2007). Mindset: The new psychology of success. Ballantine Books.

Chapter 7

page 62 *then the Authenticity stage enables you to create your own:* While many developmental theories describe this stage, the use of the term *authenticity* comes from the work of Jenny Wade, author of Changes of Mind: A Holonomic Theory of the Evolution of Consciousness. State University of New York (1996).

Chapter 8

page 78 *emotions result from times when our brain made an incorrect prediction:* Barrett, Lisa Feldman. How Emotions Are Made: The Secret Life of the Brain (p. 66). Houghton Mifflin Harcourt.

Chapter 9

page 83 *As psychologist Mona Delahooke describes:* Delahooke, M. (2019). Beyond behaviors: Using brain science and compassion to understand and solve children's behavioral challenges (Chapter 2). PESI Publishing & Media.

How Are They Sleeping?

page 84 *most adolescents need nine to ten hours of sleep per night:* Johns Hopkins Medicine. (n.d.). *Teenagers and sleep: How much sleep is enough?* https://www.hopkinsmedicine.org/health/wellness-and-prevention /teenagers-and-sleep-how-much-sleep-is-enough

page 84 *Those who consistently get less sleep:* Wheaton, A. G., Chapman, D. P., & Croft, J. B. (2016). School start times, sleep, behavioral, health, and academic outcomes: A review of the literature. *Journal of School Health, 86*(5), 363–381. https://doi.org/10.1111/josh.12388

page 85 *leads adolescents to have a shifting body clock:* Roenneberg, T. et al. (2004). A marker for the end of adolescence. *Current Biology, 14*(24), R1038–R1039.

page 85 *until the effect peaks somewhere in their late teens to age twenty:* Roenneberg, T. et al. (2004). A marker for the end of adolescence. *Current Biology, 14*(24), R1038–R1039.

page 85 *sleeping in only on the weekends does not:* Zhang, J., Paksarian, D., Lamers, F., Hickie, I. B., He, J., & Merikangas, K. R. (2017). Sleep patterns and mental health correlates in US adolescents. *Journal of Pediatrics*, *182*, 137–143. https://doi.org/10.1016/j.jpeds.2016.11.007. ISSN 0022-3476.

page 85 *The American Pediatric Association recommends:* Adolescent Sleep Working Group; Committee on Adolescence; Council on School Health. (2014). School start times for adolescents. *Pediatrics*, *134*(3), 642–649.

page 86 *A staggering 66 percent of adolescents in the US are chronically sleep-deprived:* Tarokh, L., Saletin, J. M., & Carskadon, M. A. (2016). Sleep in adolescence: Physiology, cognition, and mental health. *Neuroscience and Biobehavioral Reviews*, *70*, 182–188. https://doi.org/10.1016/j.neubiorev.2016.08.008. *And* Eaton, D. K., McKnight-Eily, L. R., Lowry, R., Perry, G. S., Presley-Cantrell, L., & Croft, J. B. (2010, Apr.). Prevalence of insufficient, borderline, and optimal hours of sleep among high school students–United States, 2007. *Journal of Adolescent Health*, *46*(4), 399–401. https://doi.org/10.1016/j.jadohealth.2009.10.011 [Epub 2010, Jan. 4]. PMID: 20307832.

page 86 *"Insufficient sleep represents one of the most common, important, and potentially remediable health risks":* Adolescent Sleep Working Group; Committee on Adolescence; Council on School Health. (2014). School start times for adolescents. *Pediatrics*, *134*(3), 642–649. https://doi.org/10.1542/peds.2014-1697

page 87 *Set a bedtime of 10 P.M. or earlier:* Gangwisch, J. E., Babiss, L. A., Malaspina, D., Turner, J. B., Zammit, G. K., & Posner, K. (2010, Jan.). Earlier parental set bedtimes as a protective factor against depression and suicidal ideation. *Sleep*, *33*(1), 97–106. https://doi.org/10.1093/sleep/33.1.97. PMID: 20120626. PMCID: PMC2802254.

page 87 *If they consume caffeine:* Buxton, O. M., Chang, A. M., Spilsbury, J. C., Bos, T., Emsellem, H., & Knutson, K. L. (2015). Sleep in the modern family: Protective family routines for child and adolescent sleep. *Sleep Health*, *1*(1), 15–27. https://doi.org/10.1016/j.sleh.2014.12.002

page 87 *Have consistent mealtimes:* Illingworth, G. (2020). The challenges of adolescent sleep. *Interface Focus*, *10*(3), 20190080. https://doi.org/10.1098/rsfs.2019.0080

page 87 *Stop any screen time thirty to sixty minutes before bed:* Perrault, A. A., Bayer, L., Peuvrier, M., Afyouni, A., Ghisletta, P., Brockmann, C.,

Spiridon, M., Hulo Vesely, S., Haller, D. M., Pichon, S., Perrig, S., Schwartz, S., & Sterpenich, V. (2019, Sep.). Reducing the use of screen electronic devices in the evening is associated with improved sleep and daytime vigilance in adolescents. *Sleep, 42*(9), zsz125. https://doi.org /10.1093/sleep/zsz125. PMID: 31260534.

page 87 *Use light exposure:* Illingworth, G. (2020). The challenges of adolescent sleep. *Interface Focus, 10*(3), 20190080. https://doi.org/10.1098 /rsfs.2019.0080

What Are Their Senses Telling Them?

page 88 *we assume too many behaviors are top-down:* Delahooke, M. (2019). Beyond behaviors: Using brain science and compassion to understand and solve children's behavioral challenges (Chapter 2). PESI Publishing & Media.

page 89 *our sensitivities are a form of intelligence:* Shepherd, P. (2017). Radical wholeness [Kindle edition] (p. 113). North Atlantic Books.

How Are They Eating?

page 89 *neuroscientist Lisa Feldman Barrett makes a powerful point:* Barrett, L. F. (2017). How emotions are made: The secret life of the brain (p. 176). Houghton Mifflin Harcourt.

page 90 *Middle school is the time of greatest emotional volatility in our lives:* Larson, R. W., Moneta, G., Richards, M. H., & Wilson, S. (2002, July– Aug.). Continuity, stability, and change in daily emotional experience across adolescence. *Child Development, 73*(4), 1151–1165. https://doi .org/10.1111/1467-8624.00464. PMID: 12146740.

page 90 *foods that cause less variation in our blood sugar levels:* Micha, R., Rogers, P. J., & Nelson, M. (2011, Nov.). Glycaemic index and glycaemic load of breakfast predict cognitive function and mood in school children: A randomised controlled trial. *British Journal of Nutrition, 106*(10), 1552–1561. https://doi.org/10.1017/S0007114511002303 [Epub 2011, June 8]. PMID: 21736777.

page 90 *Food that has higher nutrient value, is less processed:* O'Neil, A., Quirk, S. E., Housden, S., Brennan, S. L., Williams, L. J., Pasco, J. A., Berk, M., & Jacka, F. N. (2014). Relationship between diet and mental health in children and adolescents: A systematic review. *American Journal of Public Health, 104*(10) e31–e42. https://doi.org/10.2105/AJPH.2014.302110

page 91 *As Education Week wrote:* Prothero, A. (2019, Oct. 14). Why 20-minute lunch periods aren't good for students. *Education Week.* Retrieved from www.edweek.org.

page 91 *Research points to lengthening school lunchtime:* Bergman, E. et al. (2004, Fall). The relationship between the length of the lunch period and nutrient consumption in the elementary school lunch setting. *Journal of Child Nutrition & Management, 28*(2). *And* Cohen, J. F. W. et al. (2016). Amount of time to eat lunch is associated with children's selection and consumption of school meal entrée, fruits, vegetables, and milk. *Journal of the Academy of Nutrition and Dietetics, 116*(1), 123–128.

page 91 *having family meals together leads to better eating:* Hammons, A. J., & Fiese, B. H. (2011). Is frequency of shared family meals related to the nutritional health of children and adolescents? *Pediatrics, 127*(6), e1565–e1574. https://doi.org/10.1542/peds.2010-1440

How Are They Moving?

page 92 *better sleep quality:* Lang, C., Brand, S., Feldmeth, A. K., Holsboer-Trachsler, E., Pühse, U., & Gerber, M. (2013, Aug. 15). Increased self-reported and objectively assessed physical activity predict sleep quality among adolescents. *Physiology & Behavior, 120,* 46–53. https://doi.org/10.1016/j.physbeh.2013.07.001 [Epub 2013, July 9]. PMID: 23851332.

page 92 *better mental health:* Rodriguez-Ayllon, M. et al. (2019, Sep.). Role of physical activity and sedentary behavior in the mental health of preschoolers, children, and adolescents: A systematic review and meta-analysis. *Sports Medicine, 49*(9), 1383–1410. https://doi.org/10.1007/s40279-019-01099-5. PMID: 30993594.

page 92 *improvements in their cognitive abilities:* Hatch, L. M., Dring, K. J., Williams, R. A., Sunderland, C., Nevill, M. E., & Cooper, S. B. (2021, Nov. 4). Effect of differing durations of high-intensity intermittent activity on cognitive function in adolescents. *International Journal of Environmental Research and Public Health, 18*(21), 11594. https://doi.org/10.3390/ijerph182111594. PMID: 34770104. PMCID: PMC8583632.

page 92 *particularly positive effect on the cognitive abilities known as executive function:* Best, J. R. (2010, Dec.). Effects of physical activity on children's executive function: Contributions of experimental research on aerobic exercise. *Developmental Review, 30*(4), 331–551. https://doi.org /10.1016/j.dr.2010.08.001. PMID: 21818169. PMCID: PMC3147174.

Bringing It All Together

page 94 *In a Canadian study looking at lifestyle recommendations for early adolescents:* Loewen, O. K., Maximova, K., Ekwaru, J. P., Faught, E. L., Asbridge, M., Ohinmaa, A., & Veugelers, P. J. (2019, May). Lifestyle behavior and mental health in early adolescence. *Pediatrics, 143*(5), e20183307. https://doi.org/10.1542/peds.2018-3307

Chapter 10

page 98 *In study after study:* Durlak, J. A., Weissberg, R. P., Dymnicki, A. B., Taylor, R. D., & Schellinger, K. (2011). The impact of enhancing students' social and emotional learning: A meta-analysis of school-based universal interventions. *Child Development, 82*, 405–432. *And* Taylor, R. D., Oberle, E., Durlak, J. A., & Weissberg, R. P. (2017). Promoting positive youth development through school-based social and emotional learning interventions: A meta-analysis of follow-up effects. *Child Development, 88*, 1156–1171. https://doi.org/10.1111/cdev.12864. For further research and recent updates, see the research database maintained by CASEL (The Collaborative for Academic, Social, and Emotional Learning) at www.casel.org.

page 99 *think of these skills as being in four categories:* This four-part framework is drawn from the Anchorage School District PK–12 Social and Emotional Learning Standards, retrieved at https://www.asdk12.org/Page/6643.

page 102 *Intriguing research shows that the more clear and specific our language around emotions:* Barrett, L. F. (2017). *How emotions are made: The secret life of the brain* (pp. 182–183). Houghton Mifflin Harcourt. *And* Smidt, K. E., & Suvak, M. K. (2015). A brief, but nuanced, review of emotional granularity and emotion differentiation research. *Current Opinion in Psychology, 3*, 48–51. https://doi.org/10.1016/j.copsyc.2015 .02.007. ISSN 2352-250X.

Chapter 11

page **106** *this is inherently a socially focused time:* See research and references in Chapter 1 notes.

page **107** *facial expressions in particular:* Steinberg, L. (2014). Age of opportunity: Lessons from the new science of adolescence (p. 95). Houghton Mifflin Harcourt.

page **111** *developed a framework of seven ways:* Nesi, J., Choukas-Bradley, S., & Prinstein, M. J. (2018). Transformation of adolescent peer relations in the social media context: Part 2—Application to peer group processes and future directions for research. Clinical Child and Family Psychology Review, 21(3), 295–319. https://doi.org/10.1007/s10567-018-0262-9

page **113** *Research shows that direct communication online:* Verduyn, P., Lee, D. S., Park, J., Shablack, H., Orvell, A., Bayer, J., Ybarra, O., Jonides, J., & Kross, E. (2015). Passive Facebook usage undermines affective well-being: Experimental and longitudinal evidence. Journal of Experimental Psychology: General, 144(2), 480–488. https://doi.org/10.1037/xge0000057. **And** Hamilton, J. L., Do, Q. B., Choukas-Bradley, S., Ladouceur, C. D., & Silk, J. S. (2021). Where it hurts the most: Peer interactions on social media and in person are differentially associated with emotional reactivity and sustained affect among adolescent girls. Research on Child and Adolescent Psychopathology, 49(2), 155–167. https://doi.org/10.1007/s10802-020-00725-5

Chapter 12

page **120** *Dunbar's number:* Dunbar, R. I. M. (1992). Neocortex size as a constraint on group size in primates. *Journal of Human Evolution, 22*(6), 469–493. ISSN 0047-2484.

page **120** *Author Malcolm Gladwell famously told the story of the company Gore-Tex:* Gladwell, M. (2002). *The tipping point: How little things can make a big difference.* Back Bay Books.

page **121** *Research on small schools:* Lee, V. E., & Loeb, S. (2000). School size in Chicago elementary schools: Effects on teachers' attitudes and students' achievement. *American Educational Research Journal, 37*(1), 3–31.

page **122** *As the science of learning has progressed:* Darling-Hammond, L., Flook, L., Cook-Harvey, C., Barron, B., & Osher, D. (2020). Implications for educational practice of the science of learning and development. *Applied Developmental Science, 24*(2), 97–140. https://doi.org/10.1080/10888691.2018.1537791

page 126 *what Stanford professor Denise Pope calls PDF:* Pope, D., & Brown, M. et al. (2015). *Overloaded and underprepared: Strategies for stronger schools and healthy, successful kids.* John Wiley & Sons.

page 127 *American teachers spend significantly more hours in front of students:* Burns, D., & Darling-Hammond, L. (2014). *Teaching around the world: What can TALIS tell us?* Stanford Center for Opportunity Policy in Education. *And* Walker, T. D. (2016, Sep.). The ticking clock of teacher burnout. *The Atlantic.*

Chapter 13

page 133 *target fixation:* Target fixation. (2022, Apr. 15). In *Wikipedia*, https://en.wikipedia.org/w/index.php?title=Target_fixation&oldid=1005550974

page 133 *first identified in World War II:* Colgan, W. B. (2010). *Allied strafing in World War II: A cockpit view of air to ground battle* (p. 44). McFarland. ISBN 978-0-7864-4887-6.

page 134 *first bring to mind the anchoring effect:* Furnham, A., & Boo, H. C. (2011). A literature review of the anchoring effect. *Journal of Socio-Economics, 40*(1), 35–42. https://doi.org/10.1016/j.socec.2010.10.008. ISSN 1053-5357.

page 136 *they find the entire school on the field:* Athenian School, in Danville, California (www.athenian.org).

page 142 *many recent studies have found no correlation between video game use and aggression:* Przybylski, A. K., & Weinstein, N. (2019). Violent video game engagement is not associated with adolescents' aggressive behaviour: Evidence from a registered report. *Royal Society Open Science, 6,* 171474. *And* Ferguson, C. J., Rueda, S. M., Cruz, A. M., Ferguson, D. E., Fritz, S., & Smith, S. M. (2008). Violent video games and aggression: Causal relationship or byproduct of family violence and intrinsic violence motivation? *Criminal Justice and Behavior, 35*(3), 311–332. https://doi.org/10.1177/0093854807311719. *And* Kühn, S., Kugler, D., Schmalen, K. et al. (2019). Does playing violent video games cause aggression? A longitudinal intervention study. *Molecular Psychiatry*, *24*, 1220–1234. https://doi.org/10.1038/s41380-018-0031-7

page 143 *what psychologist Jean Piaget termed the "concrete" stage:* See research and references in Appendix 1: Developmental Research.

page 144 *exercises with cognitive complexity:* Best, J. R. (2010, Dec.). Effects of physical activity on children's executive function: Contributions of experimental research on aerobic exercise. *Developmental Review*, *30*(4), 331–551. https://doi.org/10.1016/j.dr.2010.08.001. PMID: 21818169. PMCID: PMC3147174.

page 149 *As author Michelle Icard writes:* Icard, M. (2016). *Middle school makeover* (p. 61). Taylor & Francis.

Chapter 16

page 185 *you could ask the person sharing if they would like responses of empathy, advice, or questions:* This is inspired by the Open Session technique developed at the Institute for Social & Emotional Learning (https://www.instituteforsel.net/).

Chapter 17

page 192 *information with more emotional content is retained better:* Stenson, A. F., Leventon, J. S., & Bauer, P. J. (2019). Emotion effects on memory from childhood through adulthood: Consistent enhancement and adult gender differences. *Journal of Experimental Child Psychology*, *178*, 121–136.

Chapter 18

page 203 *Some modern-day writers even:* Drucker, P. (1993, Spring). The rise of the knowledge society. *Wilson Quarterly*, *17*(2), 63–65.

page 204 *"It is only through enforced standardization . . . ":* Taylor, F. W. (1911). *The principles of scientific management* (Chapter 2). Harper & Brothers.

page 204 *disproven by modern learning science:* Darling-Hammond, L., Flook, L., Cook-Harvey, C., Barron, B., & Osher, D. (2020). Implications for educational practice of the science of learning and development. *Applied Developmental Science*, *24*(2), 97–140. https://doi.org/10.1080/10888691.2018.1537791

page 206 *the research that longer lunches lead students to eat more healthfully:*
Bergman, E. et al. (2004, Fall). The relationship between the length of
the lunch period and nutrient consumption in the elementary school
lunch setting. *Journal of Child Nutrition & Management, 28*(2). *And*
Cohen, J. F. W. et al. (2016). Amount of time to eat lunch is associated
with children's selection and consumption of school meal entrée, fruits,
vegetables, and milk. *Journal of the Academy of Nutrition and Dietetics,
116*(1), 123–128.

page 206 *which support better adolescent mental and physical health:* Adolescent Sleep Working Group; Committee on Adolescence; Council on
School Health. (2014). School start times for adolescents. *Pediatrics,
134*(3), 642–649. https://doi.org/10.1542/peds.2014-1697

Chapter 19

page 215 *Jiyu Gakuen:* Author's personal experience. For more information,
see https://www.jiyu.ac.jp/.

page 216 *Evangelische Schule Berlin Zentrum (ESBZ):* Author's personal experience. For more information, see https://www.ev-schule-zentrum.de/, as
well as the profile of ESBZ in Frederic Laloux's book *Reinventing Organizations: A Guide to Creating Organizations Inspired by the Next Stage in
Human Consciousness* (Nelson Parker, 2014).

page 216 *Millennium School:* Author's personal experience. For more
details, see www.millenniumschool.org.

page 217 *Argonaut:* Author's personal experience. For more details, see
www.argonaut.school.

page 218 *the anchoring effect:* Furnham, A., & Boo, H. C. (2011). A literature review of the anchoring effect. *Journal of Socio-Economics, 40*(1),
35–42. https://doi.org/10.1016/j.socec.2010.10.008. ISSN 1053-5357.

Appendix 1: Developmental Research

page 233 *Michael Commons:* Commons, M. L. (2007). Introduction to
the model of hierarchical complexity. *Behavioral Development Bulletin,
13*(1), 1–6. https://doi.org/10.1037/h0100493. ISSN 1942-0722.

NOTES

page 233 *Susanne Cook-Greuter:* Cook-Greuter, S. (2021). *Ego development: A full-spectrum theory of vertical growth and meaning making.* Retrieved via www.researchgate.net.

page 234 *Robert Kegan:* Kegan, R. (1994). *In over our heads: The mental demands of modern life.* Harvard University Press.

page 234 *Lawrence Kohlberg:* Kohlberg, L. & Hersh, R. H. (1977). Moral development: A review of the theory. *Theory into Practice, 16*(2), 53–59. https://doi.org/10.1080/00405847709542675

page 234 *Abraham Maslow:* Maslow, A. H. (1943). A theory of human motivation. *Psychological Review, 50*(4), 370–396. https://doi.org/10.1037/h0054346

page 234 *Jean Piaget:* Piaget, J. (1971). The theory of stages in cognitive development. In D. R. Green, M. P. Ford, & G. B. Flamer (Eds.), *Measurement and Piaget.* McGraw-Hill.

page 234 *Jenny Wade:* Wade, J. (1996). *Changes of mind: A holonomic theory of the evolution of consciousness.* State University of New York.

page 235 *Ken Wilber:* Wilber, K. (2000). *Integral psychology: Consciousness, spirit, psychology, therapy.* Shambhala.

page 235 *Thich Nhat Hanh described it most compellingly:* Nhat Hanh, T. (2006). *Understanding our mind.* Parallax Press.

INDEX